'Thought provoking! Mind grabbing! Everyone I know should own a copy of this book.' – *Chief Roy Wilson, Spiritual Leader of the Cowlitz Tribe and author of **Medicine Wheels**.*

'Is it time for you to wake up? This book offers you gentle passage into fuller consciousness through your own knowing heart. Your spirit is calling you. Do you hear it?

Help yourself by listening to one woman's voice as she models the integrity of following her own path and listening to her own guidance.

This honest book, loaded with memorable gems and the simplicity of a life consciously lived, offers the wisdom of the grandmothers.' – *praise from Anne Katherine, author of bestselling book, **Boundaries: Where You End and I Begin.***

STOP!

Do not go any further if you're looking
for a self-help book or an instruction manual;
you will not find it here.

There are no steps to follow
only words on paper,
words from my heart to yours.

But if you are willing to listen
with the eyes and ears of your heart
this book is for you.

Let everything else blow with the wind!

I Believe In You

Discovering the Inside Passage
to Happiness

by

Sandy Powers

BARB,
It took an inner
strength i courage to live your
true self, to work the program,
to mature into a woman who
shines love. May you find
the hidden treasure within
these words... you.
d

Sandy Powers, P.O. Box 815, Lake Stevens, WA 98258
www.sandypowers.com

Powers, Sandy, 1955-
I Believe In You: Discovering the Inside Passage to Happiness
Includes bibliographical references.

Library of Congress Control Number: 2006904848

ISBN 978-0-9785838-0-4
1.Spiritual life 2. Inspirational 3. Happiness

Printed in the United States of America

Dedicated to my great, great, great grandchild.

ACKNOWLEDGEMENTS

My deepest gratitude goes to Shirley Murphy who offered to underwrite the printing cost of this book before it was finished. Shirley, you are one of God's angels on Earth; to my father Gordon Stewart for spending countless hours editing my many attempts to get it right. I am grateful for your red pen, but most of all for our relationship; to my husband Joe Powers, my true love and anchor; to my children, DJ, Desirae, and Ryan, who listen to their hearts and add to this world in incredible ways; to my incredible friends Ycenna Finnigan, Jackie Reynolds, Vicki Ellen, Star Walker, Teri Eberlien, and Mark Donohue who tell me what I know when I forget; to my original Listening to Life group, Laurie Harville, Anna Matysik, Amy Masson, Pearl Bjodstrup, Diane Nichols, Eney Gaines Winkle, Patricia Doyle, Jill Rosendal, powerful women I met under an oak tree a long time ago and Linda LaBell who adds so much to this world; to my mentors born a generation before, who've touched my life deeply, Dema Howard, Florence Sibley, Mary Butler, and Gayle McNicol and my beautiful Grandma Marshall for holding me when I needed it most; to my siblings Gordon, Robyn, and Stacey. Without our dance I wouldn't be who I am. I love you; to my mother Georgi Schweitzer who gave birth to me twice, once when I was born and then again when she died. She taught me to grab the brass ring when it comes around and find humor hidden in the pocket of every experience. I love you, Mom; to Roy Wilson for his wisdom and supporting this project; to my editor, Jeri Nilsen, for tying the ribbon around the package.

AUTHOR'S NOTE

We come from the same source, yet we are a unique expression of that source.

No one else has lived our lives. We are all different. We have different beliefs. We have different religious expressions. We come from different parts of the world. We have our own cultural understandings. We look different. Differences enhance the whole.

By honoring our differences the thread that connects us all is revealed.

WAYS TO USE THIS BOOK

INDIVIDUALS

Pick a section at random, or find an essay title that resonates with you, or start at the beginning and read to the end. After you read a section roll it over in your heart and ask, what story of my own did it bring to mind, why did I pick this essay at this time, what may it be suggesting to me? Then journal your discoveries.

FRIENDS SHARING

Do the same as individual directions but share your discoveries with each other.

GROUPS

Pick an essay and share your discoveries with each other. Questions to start the discussion might be - What story of your own did you relate to the essay? How did your story shift after reading this section? How might your discovery serve you and/or those around you? Your stories and discoveries shared will serve the group.

Most importantly take your time; there is no rush. These pages are here to serve you.
Reach behind the words and discover the treasure you seek.

Have fun.
Sandy Powers

CONTENTS

Acknowledgments i
Author's Note ii
Forward vi

Turmoil 1
Calling 5
Holy Work 9
Walk the Talk 11
Acceptance 15
Truth 17
Heaven 19
Obstacles 23
Discovering 25
Emotional Pain 27
Partners 29
Internal Gauge 31
Sacred Unwinding 33
Death 35
Being a Vagabond 39
Doubt 43
Taking It Slower 49
Coincidences 51
Separate or Connected 57
Big Belly Laughs 59
Know Thy Self 61
Entering the Past 63
Commitment to Heal 69
Weight 73
Heroes 75
Value 79
Daily Living 81
Grief 83
Change 85

Spiritual Practice 87
Faith 89
Intuition 91
Silence 93
Confidence 95
Risking 101
Meditation 105
Forgiveness 107
Parenting... 113
Reasons... 115
Observing 117
Questioning God 121
Action 125
Progress 127
Ageless 129
Discernment.. 133
Unknown... 135
Time 143
I Know That 149
Healing 151
Everything Serves 155
Listening to Life 159
Making Space 165
Happiness 167
Connecting to Truth 171
Answers... 173
From One Mother to Another 175
Awareness 179
Adding Good Things 181
Turning Fifty 185
Listening 189
Perceptions 191
Starting Again 195

Conclusion... *x*
Afterword .... *xi*
Endnotes .... *xii*
One Lingering Question .... *xvi*

FORWARD

Looking back through the history of the human race we become aware of so much pain that has existed and quite possibly the greatest pain is part of our current scene. Pain begins with the individual therefore the healing must also begin with the individual.

This is what Sandy's mind-grabbing, thought-provoking, book is all about - healing for the individual. She accomplishes this through introspection into her own life, giving us examples. She reveals how she delves into the most tender of her pains in this heart-throbbing story.

Sandy teaches us that observing both the obvious and the obscure and accepting yourself and your own potential, moves you into the next phase of living.

Being at one with her own life, exposing the negatives of her own experiences as well as the positives, gives us much needed inspiration.

I would like all my friends to read and take advantage of the lessons in this exceptional book on self-healing.

Roy I. Rochon Wilson
September 2006

I Believe In You

Discovering the Inside Passage
to Happiness

TURMOIL

For we are, actually, pioneers trying to find a new path
through the maze of tradition, convention and dogma.

Anne Morrow Lindbergh – Gift from the Sea

QUESTIONS drag me along on a leash. Sometimes I don't want to go but I get pulled forward little by little. Every now and then a big old yank comes out of nowhere almost breaking my neck, usually when I'm sniffing my business for too long.

There are times I seek solitude. I don't want to talk or visit or do anything. I'm bored. I need to be quiet and be with myself completely alone. When I'm in one of my barren tree trunk phases I struggle to find balance.

Am I too needy? Am I lazy? What is wrong? I have so much to be thankful for. Why am I so down? Why can't I sit still and let this phase have its turn?

Part of the answer boils down to no exercise. I'm sure of it. On icy days I don't want to go to the gym. My house is cold. I don't want to get up and run up and down my stairs for fifteen minutes or put on an exercise tape. All I want to do is stay in bed where it's toasty warm.

When I make it out of bed I stand shivering at the bathroom sink brushing my teeth. I turn on the shower, rinse my mouth, and hop back in bed to wait until I see a cloud of steam above the shower stall. Hot water. Yes.

I dash back into the bathroom, jump in the shower, close the door, and stand. My head and body are immersed under

1

the falling sun. I wish I had a rotating floor so I wouldn't have to keep turning around trying to keep every part of me warm.

When I dress I put a scarf around my neck, pull on my long pants, dive wet head into my shirt, and step into my sheepskin slippers. Our heat costs a fortune so I rarely turn it on. Instead I sit at my computer and turn on the small heater I have under my desk by my feet.

Winters are tough on a lot of people, but I don't mind them. I was born November 1955 in the Midwest. That meant sitting outside wrapped up in a snowsuit while my mother sat inside smoking a cigarette watching me. Why? Because Dr. Spock said one hour of fresh air a day is mandatory for every baby. Now I don't know if that's why I like winter, but it makes for a good story.

I'm a great hibernator.

'Patient for all that is unresolved in my heart' is what Rilke suggests. Now that's a challenge. Live in the moment. Let life happen.

Let it be, let it go, still the mind, reach inside, shake it loose. How do I do that? How do I do **that**, and not have to do **that** again? I don't. Dealing with Life is ongoing. Either I hear the whistle blow and get on board or watch the train pass by wondering where everyone's going.

Peeling an onion. This analogy has been used forever to describe the layers of our own discoveries. Just when we think we're there, we are and we're not. After a good onion peeling I take time to wipe my eyes and rinse my face.

I need a big breather before diving into another layer of my life. To integrate my discoveries and soak in what I've learned I need time. Time I share with big belly laughs and being silly.

How do I know when it's time to peel another layer or, as they say, hit the trail again?

I start feeling out of balance. My son says the feeling 'is like he's using again when he's not'. I'm more angry than not, more anxious than not, more uncomfortable than not. I seek solitude to see where I'm at. If I take the time, I know.

CALLING

Let us become the change we seek in this world.

Mahatma Gandhi

INNER work is something I do to stay sane. I have friends who do different things to stay connected to their hearts. I do what I do.

When I want to paint I see my friend who is passionate about painting. When I want to learn more about gardening I see my friend whose hands are at home in the dirt. When my friends want to explore their inner landscape they see me.

Serving in our own way life expresses through us. A mentor once asked me about an obstacle she was dealing with. I was surprised because I was usually the one asking questions. When I questioned her about questioning me she said, 'Why would I waste my time trying to figure out what is so easy for you?'

We are born to serve in a way no one else on Earth can. Life wanted to see itself expressed through us, to experience us serving the greater good.

We each carry a pair of shoes given to us before birth. Cinderella had her glass slippers and we have ours. When we own our gift, our unique calling, it means we've put on our shoes. Doors open and things begin to happen.

Faith is alive when we step into our calling. Not only does Life support us, we receive everything we need for the journey. Our job is to stay aligned with our hearts and do whatever it takes to hear the still small voice.

I stepped into my shoes when I turned fifty. My life is about listening and encouraging others to be the best they can be. That ability was part of me when I took my first breath, I just wasn't aware of it.

Did I know the exact form my calling would take? No. Was that unnerving? Yes, it was.

What I did know, Life would take care of me no matter what. I was determined to live my calling despite the financial stability I was used to. The form it takes is up to God; the willingness to live that form is up to me.

To keep myself on track I have a daily practice. Part of that practice is to watch myself to make sure I'm not pulling back the reins and trying to control my life. When I get anxious or overwhelmed with all the uncertainties I pull my senses back in to my heart and reconnect with the calm at my core. I hear the still small voice say, 'Walk your heart, you cannot fail.'

Walking my heart focuses me inward to where, as Evelyn Underhill author of *The Mystic Way* puts it, the indwelling Spirit of Love takes care of me. When I walk the heart I'm in tune with the Great Mystery.

Sometimes I envision being carried on the back of an eagle. I'm nestled between two feathery shoulder blades, cozy in the warmth surrounding me. We are flying high in the sky. The sun is shining and the wind is gentle on my face. All I do is look at blue sky and small puffy white clouds scattered here and there. The eagle takes me where I need to go; I don't have to worry. When I climbed on board I turned over all decisions to the eagle. When we get there all I have to do is be myself. His will is my will as my will is his. When I walk my heart I cannot fail.

HOLY WORK

Within every person is the capacity to become
something greater than he now is.

Paul McElroy.

W RITERS help me to understand myself. They help calm the chaos inside me. When their words resonate with my heart I get excited to turn the page. I've always wondered what writing did for the author. Now I know.

I watched my father, at seventy-three, step into the writer shoes he was born to wear. I watched him shift as he expressed himself differently. He seemed happier, more verbal with his feelings, and he appeared eager to serve in ways I never imagined my father serving. Even my husband noticed.

I wonder if this is how we all get when we begin to live our purpose?

An email I sent my father after reflecting on his unique vocation reads:

> Dad,
>   It's interesting where your writing has taken you lately. When I peek under the words you write, it appears you are taking snippets of emotions and playing them out, allowing your characters to process aspects of yourself you don't talk about.

I like you as a person the more I experience the other hats you wear. You have a genuine heart and are living it more each day.

You seem to have opened up to your unique vocation. Folks in my line of work refer to it as 'holy work', for you it is the role of a writer. It appears the more you believe in yourself and your gift the more compelled you are to explore.

There's an inner peace that comes with this type of discovery. I bet all your relationships are changing. You're different, a good different. Even Joe has noticed a shift in you. He likes what he sees and says he feels closer to you now.

As you discover new layers of yourself characters surface bringing those discoveries to life. As they deal with things they seem to get dealt with in you. It's a win/win for everyone. Your readers win because they can relate to the characters and you win because you let loose what needs to be let loose.

That is a sign of 'Holy Work', it's a win/win for everyone.

Love you
S

My father emailed a simple reply, thank you dear.

WALK THE TALK

Good words do not give me back my children.

Chief Joseph, Nez Perce

WORDS are nothing unless backed up by action. My talk must show up in my actions. If it doesn't, I go looking for it.

How many times have we been hurt by broken promises? How many promises have we broken?

We've all let others down and they've let us down. We're human. When my children broke a promise I'd ask them to show me I can trust them again.

It is the same for me. If I can't walk the talk, I should keep my mouth shut. Speak less, do more. Easier said than done.

The best teaching I can give those around me won't come from the words I speak. It will come from the life I live. Am I living what I believe?

It's easy to get caught up in the energy of those around us. I work on not talking about people in a negative light. There are days I fail. I'm getting better. I catch myself sooner, but it's still a challenge.

We live in a society filled with gossip. I grew up in a household that got excited about the weekly gossip magazines. It was a cheap form of entertainment. We had fun sitting on my mom's bed, my brother, sister, and I, each of us reading the latest, greatest, gossip floating around Hollywood.

11

Since I was a kid talking about someone else has been the social norm. Eventually conversations turn to someone not present, and more often than not, the talk isn't very nice. Comments are made, opinions spouted, and before long I'd catch myself chiming in whether I knew the person or not. I'd be agreeing and nodding my head.

When I finally realized my habitual obsession I challenged myself to shift hurtful conversations to love. When I'm around a conversation that's turning nasty I jump in and make a positive comment about that person, or joke about my own imperfections.

Sometimes that works and other times I get a dirty look and they continue right where they left off. Other times I remain silent or leave the room depending on my energy level. And I hate to say it, there are times when I start the hurtful conversation.

When I do I feel awful. I've learned doing and saying things I regret later is tied directly to self-care. Before going into social settings I try to remember to check my energy level. If I'm on low then I better not go, or leave early, and definitely talk less.

Walking the talk takes energy. It's living the love in your heart. Living love sounds easy but breaking habits that we've grown up with that we thought were socially acceptable such as gossiping, is hard.

Dancing to my own drum and singing my own song takes discipline. My way is off the beaten path, but it makes me happy. I want my children to discover their own beliefs and understandings, and live them, too.

Being a parent and allowing my children to walk their talk is tough. When they express their ideas I get excited, but my excitement is usually followed by caution, wanting to control how that idea takes form.

Why do I have trouble letting them follow their hearts and taking the steps they want to take? I'm older and wiser, aren't I? My way is safer, isn't it?

When I try to control my adult children from what I perceive as potential failures or financial disasters, I realize it is fear talking.

I have no power over my children. No matter how much I wish I did at times, that power belongs to them. They've owned it all along. My job is to love and support them as they discover their power and use it to turn their dreams into reality.

Since the day I first laid eyes on them I prayed they would listen to their own hearts and discover their greatness. Mistakes are needed. Those very mistakes possess gifts and opportunities that lead to the next step. My strongest teaching is to walk my talk and live my life fully.

ACCEPTANCE

In knowing how to overcome little things, a centimeter
at a time, gradually when bigger things come,
you're prepared.

Katherine Dunham – I Dream A World –
Interview by Brian Lanker

SHE didn't preach. She practiced. That's what Gayle told me when I asked about her mother.

'During the Depression', she said, 'hobos would come to our door and Mother would fix each one a full meal; eggs, sausage, and toast. She never turned anyone away.'

Gayle is eighty-eight years old. She says her body is wearing out. She tells me she's learned to accept every thing that comes her way.

Acceptance. Her words pierced me. I struggle with accepting the way things are. I try to change them or hurry them along. What would happen if I'd accept things the way they are and move on?

When I contemplate accepting I feel a peaceful energy spreading over me like a blanket. This is something I need more of.

She also said she quit thinking. Instead of thinking she observes her thoughts. With a giggle she added, 'I get quite a laugh out of them'.

I thanked her for being such a brilliant light in my life. I shared that even though she can't leave her house without help she's with me everyday.

'Isn't that something', she said, 'you and my granddaughter are the only ones that know me'.

'I thought you weren't thinking anymore,' I laughed. 'Every person who meets me knows you. We are part of each other.'

'I never thought of that,' she replied.

I knew she was smiling.

'I love you, Gayle.'

'I love you,' she answered in a slow calm sweet voice.

Gayle feeds me. She is an amazing woman. I can only imagine the emotions she must go through daily. I am amazed at her strength. Despite her pain she lives life from her heart accepting her age and its limitations. What a powerful teacher.

TRUTH

The most auspicious moment of your life is
when you make the commitment to know the Truth,
a commitment so firm there is no turning back.

Swami Chidvilasananda – My Lord Loves A Pure Heart

TRUTH? How do you know when something is true? Truth based on what?

When I get quiet I discover a form of Truth. I chew on it with God and ask is this Truth? When I sense a calm I know.

'Chew on it with your Heart' was a saying my kids heard growing up. Take your questions inside, not outside. Outside gives you ideas to chew on, but go inside for your answers.

Truth shakes out everywhere if I am willing to listen.

I am a vagabond. No matter what form Truth takes I am grateful for the teaching. It is like dining on fine food. I allow each morsel to nourish me. I grow more awake and alive, living life from my heart.

Many authors around the globe dine on Truth. Their words are like discovering another language for the same message. I love learning from so many sources.

'Let what feels right stick and let the rest blow with the wind' is my motto. Every book is written by human hand. Sifting through the words, Truth appears like sustenance for the weary soul. Bless all those who write from their hearts in order to serve the rest of us.

17

HEAVEN

When the words stop and you can endure the silence, That
reveals your heart's pain of emptiness or
that great wrenching-sweet longing
That is the time to try and listen to
what the Beloved's Eyes
Most want to say

Hafiz – The Gift
Poems by Hafiz - Translations by Daniel Ladinsky

MY dad once told me the only regret he'd have
when he dies is that he didn't read all the books
he wanted to read. I replied, 'Dad, what if your
heaven is a huge library in the sky, filled with all the books
you never read and you had access to discuss any of the
novels with the authors who wrote them? What if…'

He smiled. He liked that idea of heaven. Picture it, all his
books around him, sitting in a big comfy chair, good reading
light, no glasses needed. There's a big door in the library and
lots of windows. His mom and sisters drop by to say hello
before going to get a bite to eat. His kids and wife are close
by, and his dogs are at his feet-- or should I say on his lap--
okay, maybe not all at once. It would be a bit crowded. But I
like that picture of him and I'll stick with it when the time
comes.

'Why not?' is my motto. Who can prove anything, really?
Why can't we make our own heaven? Thinking up the

greatest things, who can tell us that cannot be? I haven't met anyone yet.

Theories jump like fleas in the grass, but they are only theories.

I tell my kids I believe we can create our own heaven, not only here on earth but when we die. If you can prove otherwise I might reconsider. If I'm wrong I'll be dead so what will it matter.

I used to get all worked up when I heard different versions of what happens when we die, then I realized no one really knows. Who's been there and come back? I quit believing in anyone else's version and created my own.

Who has the authority to say that if our loved ones didn't believe in a certain way we'll never see them again? Hog wash, I reply. I believe in what helps me to be a better person. If I'm wrong God and I will work it out later... I think.

I was with a friend as she was dying. Riddled with cancer, she was in the last stages of living on Earth. She was in pain but she kept hanging on. She loved her husband so much and didn't want to leave him. She worried about him. He was the love of her life.

On one of our visits she was fading in and out. One time when she came back to this world she told me what she had experienced.

She said when she left heaven she'd been with her husband. In fact they were on a ranch where they raised horses. There was a big wrap around porch where she sat with her only sister drinking coffee. They watched her husband in the corral training their horses. They ran a half-way camp for kids with problems. The kids would come out for two weeks at a time and stay with them. She said there

20

was a road a few miles away that they could see from their porch. She saw her parents drive by in their RV.

There was a peace about her. She said she knew now that even if her husband remarried, she was already with him in their heaven forever, their place in the sky. She said there were many places in heaven and if he remarries after she's gone there'll be a heaven where he and his new wife can be, too. She said we're not limited to one life in heaven, we can co-exist, or maybe more.

What a great concept. I was intrigued. What if there were different realms of existence and we could share and be with those we love simultaneously? What if?

In the last moments of her life I suggested to her husband that instead of saying it's okay to go, ask her to come to him. I knew in my heart of hearts as she left this realm she was traveling to him, into his arms, into the arms of the man she loved and lived with on another realm.

That vision will be with me always. That's what I choose to believe for Joe and me. When we die we'll die into a place where we already exist, both of us living our dreams as we did on earth. But even better, I will see my family, have my kids, have my books, have my friends, and have my parents. I will lack for nothing.

Thank you, my dear friend, for sharing your vision. It changed my life in a positive way.

OBSTACLES

If you think you can't you can't,
if you think you can you can.

Henry Ford

GETTING to the heart, the place where I do my chewing requires clearing a path and knocking down any overgrown weeds. What obstacles along my heart path need clearing?

Years ago when some one said to me, 'You are very metaphysical', I freaked. I associated metaphysical with way out there, off the wall, freaky aliens, UFOs, crystals. No, 'I'm not metaphysical,' I shot back. I had a belief wrapped around that word and I didn't want anything to do with it.

My reaction hit a nerve. What was I afraid of, more rejection? Being labeled way out there? Why was I so worried about what others thought?

Reactions get my attention. The more I watch the more I discover. A strong reaction can be an obstacle or an opportunity to question my beliefs and insecurities. Over the years I have found everything possesses a common thread, a thread the heart uses to weave the tapestry of our lives. Whatever is before me will bring me closer to God if I allow it.

I've used many different tools from many different cultures to get over obstacles. Some I still use and others I've tucked away for a rainy day. Everything has the potential to

23

bring me closer to God. Even though I may not use certain tools anymore I keep them close. You never know where life will take you next.

Meditation and prayer, reading sacred text, and walking in nature are some of my favorite tools. Mystics from all ages have used these tools to connect to the Sacred.

Obstacles are agents for transformation. They can shape-shift the form of hurtful comments, resentful feelings, painful experiences, and strong reactions. I have a choice. Either I can spiral further from my heart, becoming bitter and frustrated or I can transcend the hurdle by igniting my heart to open my eyes and ears to the gift I cannot see.

DISCOVERING

I think of many versions of Christianity, Islam, and Buddhism
now playing in the world and I wonder:
Why label? Why ask is it Christian, Muslim, Buddhist?
Why not ask simply: Is it true?

Alan Jones, PhD 'ReImagining Christianity'

OGMA. Rules. Regulations. Please. Who's right?
Who's wrong? Does love and compassion mean
nothing? Which belief is Truth? And if that belief
is Truth, is everyone else damned?

When I wake up to different aspects of myself, rubbing the
sleep out of my eyes, I can feel my wings stretch as I take
flight to see the world anew, again.

Put me in a box and seal the lid. I go crazy. My heart
whispers, 'there's more, much more, explore and discover
new ways to say the same thing. Can't you hear it, Sandy?
Listen'.

Before long I'm kicking the box apart and venturing out.
My big toe dabbling in the poetry of worlds I never knew. I
calm myself and reassure my mind of our mission. We are
following the golden thread, the divine material used by Life
to weave all of our worlds together.

Is it possible? My mind asks. I don't know, I reply.

Love is worth the effort. Weren't we all created equal?
Isn't it the same Life Force that allowed me to breathe my
first breath, the same Life Force that gave birth to every
person and thing I see?

Show me Your face in the face of those I see. Show me Your face when I look outside into the night sky. Show me Your face when I walk through the streets of the city. Let me discover You everywhere and in everything.

My friends turn on my passion. They dare to freeform to the best of their ability, opening wider, and spreading their arms around themselves learning to love in new ways.

Life is filled with new discoveries. I don't want to waste a minute.

EMOTIONAL PAIN

The highest reward for a person's toil is not what they get for
it, but what they become by it.

John Ruskin

RECOGNIZING emotional pain in others is huge.
Pain doesn't pop out in a do-it-yourself nice neat
package. It's all over the map; dirty looks, biting
words, and often, inappropriate behavior. Recognizing that
those behaviors stem from unresolved issues and pressure
cookers boiling over was a huge 'aha' moment.

Whatever they express I have inside of me too. Their
behavior is mine. Maybe I haven't taken it to that extreme or
let it out in that fashion, but it's there. Life shows me every
day why I'm on my path and why I need to roll up my
sleeves and do my own housecleaning.

When my high school aged nephew came home from
school I asked why he looked so down. In an instant he
became my guru for the day.

He said 'oh some of the kids were being really rude' and it
made him mad, it hurt his feelings, but he wasn't going to
blow up or get in a fight. He said, 'I realize they must have
been having a bad day. I knew it wasn't about me'.

At seventeen years of age I didn't know diddly, I had no
clue someone else's knife in the gut behavior was about
them and not me. I took everything personally. Hit me
again, I'd say to myself, join the club, everyone else has.

27

Quite a concept: ugly behavior shown us, is not about us, but about them.

If I can take in that possibility and not put my defenses up, how would my life look different?

Healthy boundaries. First thing that hits me is I need good boundaries. The more I heal unresolved issues and take care of the pressure cookers boiling in me, the easier it is to recognize those wounds in others.

When I lick my wounds they are tender and my toleration of others' emotional pain is lower than when my wounds have completely healed. I don't need to take on others' bad behavior, ever. If I choose to help I better make sure I have the energy to handle it.

Someone venting garbage at me takes a lot of energy to deal with. I may have the energy to listen or I may not. Sometimes it's not healthy to stay in the situation. I can't fix anyone. I can only listen. Each situation is different.

The only way I know what to do is to listen to my body. What is it telling me, flee or stay? I ask myself will it serve to stay or is it best to go? Do I have the energy to establish healthy boundaries or will staying in this situation only trigger reactions I may regret later?

Emotional pain can be explosive. It cries out to be healed. It gets our attention one way or another.

When I'm the one giving dirty looks or speaking biting words I beg Life to make me aware of those times so I may tend to my own garden and not hurt others.

PARTNERS

No man has at any time seen God. But if we love one another,
God abides in us and His love is brought to completion in us.

1 John 4:12

A client called me the other day. She was very upset
with her husband. He never talks to her. They
never communicate. She didn't know why they
were together. What was the point?

I shared with her that when I met my husband I threw all
my eggs in his basket and every day he'd promptly drop
them, leaving a goopy yucky mess all over the floor. He'd
try to carry the basket, but eggs would fall creating a disaster
everywhere.

I thought that if he was my husband he should be able to
fill all of my needs. Yeah, right. All my needs, who was I
married to, God? He didn't like to dive deep to the bottom of
the ocean and talk about all his discoveries. That's your
thing, not mine, he'd say.

He didn't get it when I shared with him an insight I
discovered. His glazed look and uh huh would make me
boil. Was I talking to a wall? Wasn't I supposed to have a
partner to share my passion with? What was wrong with us?

I'd boxed him in and he often failed. Ouch.

Then I thought, what if other people were capable of
filling that need? Wasn't that okay? What needs did he fill?
How did he serve my life? Were those things more
important than the things he didn't get?

29

I reflected on his love and his stable grounded demeanor. I thought about the big arms he'd put around me when I needed them, or how if someone hurt me he'd beat them up, that is, if I'd let him. No matter what I knew he'd stand up for me, right, wrong or indifferent. Why, because he loves me.

That he doesn't 'get' my inner world or my way of relating to the world is okay. I have friends to talk with, people to coach, strangers who appear in my life, journals where I can express my innermost thoughts. It is okay he doesn't 'get' those parts of me. I made it okay.

I had a picture in my mind of how a relationship was supposed to look and how living happily ever after shows up. What if I was wrong?

INTERNAL GAUGE

What if, as Thomas Merton insists, we harbor a hidden wholeness? What if, as the Buddhist insists, we are saturated with an innate perfection? What if, as Jesus insists, we are the light of the world? What if, as God insists, it is already good, very good?

Wayne Muller – Sabbath

BEING in a place of gratitude helps me get off my pity party, refocusing on what I have versus what I don't.

There is a time and a place to vent. I have a line inside of me, a gauge showing me when I've stepped from healthy venting into unhealthy venting. Some venting serves me and some doesn't. It's different for everyone. No one can tell me how my gauge works. Only I can determine when I'm in balance. How do I determine if my gauge is in the red zone? I have to slow down and ask myself am I out of balance?

Then I have to be willing to listen to my heart for the answer. I know how to listen. I know what is right for me and what isn't. When I remove the debris I discover my direct connection to the heart, to God and that still small voice.

I'm an ordinary woman meant to live an extraordinary life. A life where I'm happy more often than sad, a life filled with some good and some bad experiences and some great and some awful, but where survival takes a backseat behind thriving. I keep finding new ways to be happy and experience joy while being more patient with my humanness.

There is much more to me than what meets the eye. I possess realms and realms of possibilities. Regardless of my physical ability, my goal is to add to this world.

I pray to be in the moment and find the calm in any storm. Even if it looks like I'm doing nothing I know I am doing the best I can, working with what I have.

SACRED UNWINDING

There are only two ways to live your life. One is as though nothing is a miracle. The other is as though everything is a miracle.

Albert Einstein

I know Life wants me to 'get it' and tries to help me everyday. Do I always understand how it helps me? No, but I try.

One of my teachers taught me about love and life in the midst of her dying. She endured physical pain. What seemed to bother her more were her occasional bouts of emotional turmoil prompted by her inability to move. I watched and observed as my dear friend struggled to surrender to her caregivers for all of her personal needs. In that sacred unwinding she was teaching me.

Confined to a hospital bed in her home, my friend stared at a chair across the room. She turned towards me and whispered. Her words came slowly.

Pointing to the chair shoved up against the wall she whispered, 'It may be an old piece of furniture, but I've had it for over sixty years.' She told me that every time her children would come in to the room they moved it up against the wall.

She liked the chair facing a certain direction. But to her kids and other caregivers the chair was just a chair. It was in the way, so it was moved.

It made her boil, but she didn't have the energy to keep repeating her request. She said the hardest part of being physically useless was letting go of control.

After a few minutes, she continued. 'That chair takes up too much of my energy. I'm not going to spend any more time on it. I love my children. They're doing the best they can for me. Thinking about the chair is stopping me from loving them. I'm letting the chair go.'

She closed her eyes for a while, rested, and then went on. 'Letting go is a messy state of affairs, but letting go brings me closer to love. I want to spend the rest of my time loving my family. The chair has served its purpose.'

At the end of our visit I kissed her. I told her she never ceased to amaze me and that she was still teaching me about life. I told her I'd take to heart her story and work on identifying what stops me from loving and remove the barrier. Every emotion she shared and her eventual reflection gave me insight into my own journey.

Lying in a hospital bed in her living room, my friend was teaching me about letting go and love. I will be forever grateful for our friendship.

DEATH

Life is not separate from death. It only looks that way.

Blackfoot proverb

WILL I be happy with the way I've lived? Have I lived to the best of my ability? Have I treated those I love with love? How will I be remembered?

We live and we die; those two things happen. I've spent considerable time contemplating both, trying to live the way I want to be remembered.

Have I added to the world or taken from it? Have I lived life fully and passionately or have I never been satisfied? Will I know in my heart I've tried to be the best I could be? Did I find happiness? Did I experience love?

If, our life is our message, as Mahatma Gandhi says, what is my message?

Why is it when someone is dying that unresolved wounds get dumped on the table for everyone to see? What is it about death that calls forth everyone's garbage? Why does love sit quietly next to unresolved hurt at such a crucial time?

When it's my time I hope I've resolved as much as I can so I'm not a burden to others and am able to love. If not, please forgive me.

When thinking of my death, I think about my kids. I want them to realize how strong they are without me. They hold their own keys to power and strength. They possess

35

everything it takes not only to survive but also thrive in the face of any situation whether they know it or not.

I'm a tool they have used to help them discover how self-sufficient they really are. When I'm gone I know they will mourn my passing. But when they are old or going through tough times I want them to use me, to talk to me. I will be just beyond the veil, living nearer to their hearts than they realize.

I can't prove anything but if possible I will communicate through books, other people, dreams, nature-- whatever it takes-- like I always have, just in a different way. Now you see me, now you don't. Just because I'm hiding doesn't mean I'm not there. I will be with them forevermore.

I call upon those that have left this realm all the time. I imagine they are in the land of all wisdom, all knowing, and all love. If they loved me here, imagine how they can love me there. I listen in creative ways for their guidance. I read many of the spiritual authors who have passed. When I read the Bible or other spiritual books, I imagine the authors whispering their gathered collective wisdom in my ear.

It is collective wisdom woven from common threads. The ultimate Truth expressed in different ways. It excites me when I'm reading and I discover another way to say the same thing. I put that discovery in my inner pocket, ready, willing, and able to pull it out if the need ever arises.

The more I dig deep into the vast riches of the world and the thoughts of those living and dead, the more alive I feel. When I look out my window the whole world is talking to me, if I dare listen.

It's true what they say... the older you get the less you know. I realize I have studied extensively, but with each discovery is the understanding that there is even more to discover. Life keeps the flame of my passion fanned.

BEING A VAGABOND

I have shown myself to you so often and
you have not seen Me.

Muhyiddin Ibn 'Arabi

AT one time I wanted to be a spiritual director. A director sounds formal, rather commanding and in charge, but in reality a spiritual director listens and befriends, and creates an environment for the Holy Spirit to be heard.

The Holy Spirit we are told, is the still small voice inside; the one I ask to lead my life and make decisions. At times I take the helm back, intentionally or unintentionally, thinking I can do better. She doesn't care. It's my choice. She is there for me when I feel alone, my constant companion. Becoming a spiritual director ached in me for a number of years. I was sure it was what I was meant to do. But you had to be a member of a church and I wasn't.

I've tried over and over again to attend church regularly. I've thought about why being a member of a church doesn't fit with me. So far all I've discovered is church ends up feeling boxed in. Boxed in to the perceptions of a particular body of believers? I don't know, maybe more like boxed in to rules on how to live and how to be God-like.

Yet, I love going to church now and then. Occasionally, on a Sunday Joe will hear me as I wake up early and get dressed. I head out the door and get home in the early afternoon.

A church or any sacred place, on one hand calms me. The intention put into building the structure touches my heart. I love that people are gathering to get closer to God. The group intention feeds me. Yet, after attending for a while something inside of me longs for more.

I hear myself say, 'Church isn't the only place people gather to get close to God, explore.' I quit going wondering why, again? Am I avoiding being tied to one community of people? Am I avoiding the fitting in? Am I too lazy to get up and go each week? Do I want to give of my time and money to one body of God? Or, am I meant to be a vagabond?

I read a book called *The Preaching Life* by Barbara Brown Taylor. She said her calling was to work for God by getting ordained, but she suggests each of us is called for our own unique service.

She writes, 'Folks get caught up thinking that being in service to God will require them to be nicer than they already are, or to give more than they already do, or be more, to put a happy face on more often.' She asks us to ponder what if what we are doing right now is our calling to God? What if we don't have to change a thing?

I set an intention every day that whatever I do I'm doing for God. It doesn't matter what it looks like. If I ended up waiting on tables, or taking in movie tickets, or working as a receptionist, or running a fortune 500 company, would that be serving the Sacred?

What if all I need to do is switch the intention button and bring my God-serving self to the task at hand?

When I enter a classroom to teach I set an intention to serve each student to the best of my ability. I scan the room looking into the eyes of those staring at me and am thankful I get to participate in their lives.

There is no person more important than the person I'm with. I am here to serve whomever is in front of me. When I quiet my mind and focus in on this moment and whom I'm with I realize we are together for a purpose much greater than I can comprehend.

My calling is clear, concise, and ever present. I don't wonder what my purpose is, I know. But for years I pretended I didn't.

Author, Reshad Field, describes his pretending period in the prologue of his book, *The Invisible Way*. He writes, 'Often I tried to escape it and instead put my self in the hands of fate, finding my self swept along with a stream of sleep-walkers who never really inhabited this world nor saw its exquisite beauty. It was only when life became increasingly painful, and my own stupidity obvious, that I was finally able to surrender to a force much greater than myself. It was a living experience for which I forfeited my own personal life, or what I thought it was, for an uncertain outcome that has become the only possible way to live.'

I don't know if everyone else is sleep walking, but I have an insatiable desire to serve and let God unfold my life. To my struggling self who stomps her feet and wants to do something else when the road gets tough I say, get over it.

I asked Joe one night why I was so weird. What do you mean? He asked.

Most of the time I feel different from everyone else. I'm into God stuff, a lot of people aren't into that and they seem happy. How come I can't be happy unless I'm up to my neck in God?

41

He agreed that I was different that way, but he followed up with 'that's a good way'. He said I was rare. I told him I was embarrassed and felt ignorant because I didn't know dates and names of important people or events in history. But the worst part, I told him, was I didn't really care. I felt those things cluttered my mind.

I went on about how smart he is, always on top of the latest political opinions, and reminded him how frequently he catches me mispronouncing words or getting clichés turned around or singing the wrong words to a song. You know all the things people talk about at social gatherings, subjects I'm horrible at.

His response was simply, so what? He continued, 'In the big scheme of life, what good is that information? You on the other hand, he said, know what people need at exactly the right moment. You may not care about the latest political event, but you always come up with the right words when someone needs it. Now that's important work, and look at all the people you help. I look at life literally', he said, 'and you use life to help someone. See we make a good team.' He's right, we do.

DOUBT

In all your ways know, recognize, and acknowledge Him, and He
will direct and make straight and plain your paths.

Proverbs 3:6

THE clouds set in as I print out the first version of
this manuscript. Pathetic, how quickly I can jump
into the throes of poor me. Woe is me, nowhere to
take this manuscript. Why did I waste the time to write?
Who will ever read this? And if they do what good will it
do?

Frustrated, I told Joe I wish I had someone like me for me.
My whole life is about being there for others as they wake
up to their purpose and claim their unique gift. I'm there to
remind them how great they are because it seems they have
forgotten, but enough about them. Back to me.

Why don't I have a 'me' in my life? I wailed. Where's my
cheerleader to take what I write to the next level?

After twisting and turning in more shapes than a pretzel
and barking my frustration to my husband who in turn felt
totally guilty, I sat alone in my library before heading to bed.
Joe had given up and went to bed hours ago. I, on the other
hand, was determined to stay downstairs and feel sorry for
myself.

'Okay Sandy, you want some comfort', I heard the still
small voice say, 'take down one of your books off the shelf
and see if Life has anything to say to you'. I went to the top
shelf and picked out the *Tao Te Ching*, a revised version of

the book written in the 6th century BC. Holding the book in my hands I closed my eyes and said a quick prayer for just the right words to appear on the page. Then I randomly opened the book.

The first line I read jumped off the page and slapped me on the cheek while instantly bringing me back to reality. 'Wise people are not absorbed in their own needs. They take the needs of all people as their own.'

I didn't want to see that. I wanted to see, 'Poor Sandy, you're right, you deserve more.' I wanted to read 'a wise sage will be showing up at your front door tomorrow ready to take you to the next place you think you want to be.'

What did I get instead? I got a pinch, a slap, what I call 'ego alignment'. A stab of guilt pierced my ego. The book was right. Life shows me every day I have many people who support me. Every time I've needed anything help was there. The passage jolted me back to reality. It reminded me that when I'm in service all my needs are met, in fact I experience a sense of bliss.

Get your mind back on others I told myself. I chose this gig. I wasn't forced to do what I do. I have free will and choice. I've tried sleepwalking and don't like it. I see people who appear happy as clams doing what they're doing, they don't have to get into what my dad calls 'my thing', but that doesn't work for me. I tried.

I live on the edge. On the edge of *what* I sometimes wonder, reality or insanity?

I'm not sure, but over the years I've become more accepting of myself for who I am. That inner yearning to be of service is a far greater priority than the uncomfortable phases I wallow in at times.

Will I suffer greatly if I stick with who I am, different and unconventional? Will I be destitute with no income and no savings and no obvious source to make a living? What if I end up living on the streets, a burden to society? What am I fearful of?

Part of me says I'm fearful of the cultural pressure that echoes everywhere I go. If you don't have a hefty bank account and stock portfolio with assets amounting to X, you are doomed to a life of sorrow.

Am I doomed to a life of sorrow?

Sorrow filled me as soon as I asked the question. He told me, 'It doesn't matter if you have a portfolio or not. I'll hang out with you regardless of your financial status.'

How many times can I trip over myself? How many seconds are there in eternity?

When I can accept that my heart holds Truth, and have Faith, all of my needs are met. I turned my will over to the Great Mystery and in turn embraced the Almighty's will. I am led. Show me the way. Do you hear me, God? Do I hear myself?

'Open your eyes,' I hear myself say. You want more direction? Everything in life is offering you a direction and pointing the way. Open all your senses and listen. If you are willing to observe and risk and adhere to love, you'll see the life you desire is here now.

Now?

I love life even with daily struggles. The times when things are going great I make a point to stop and focus for a minute and tell myself to relish this time. I soak the good times in. I see them in my mind's eye and tell my body to absorb the moment. I tell my mind to look at my emotions

45

and enjoy how I feel. I love the good times. It feels as if I'm on vacation sipping a pineapple drink on the beach.

On the other hand, there are times I wonder if I'm really living up to my end of the stick, or should I change vocations and strive to become a master gin rummy player?

Before I jump in my car to buy a deck of playing cards, the phone rings.

A friend is calling.

When I visited her last she was going through a rough time. She lives in constant pain and they found a mass on her breast. She did the breast cancer dance ten years ago and now this. I listened to her story and let her emotional pain spew forth. When she stopped talking we looked at each other. Then I reminded her she was born for battle. I told her she had everything in her to do what needs to be done, whatever it is.

I said, 'They say some people are born warriors. They have an ability to love despite the pain they endure. That no matter what life throws their way, they have the internal makeup to withstand every blow, blows that would crush the rest of us.'

My friend is one of those warriors. Through her love she creates opportunities for happiness to grow, and love to win.

Now is that a tough gig? Did she want to quit the warrior role she's played for eighty-five years? Did she want to scream in God's face, 'why can't someone else take over, why me?' Sure. But bottom line is she was born to serve. That's her thing.

'You're probably right,' she said sighing. 'I do believe that.'

I continued. 'Even at eighty-five sitting on the island you say is getting smaller and smaller every day, you are still doing your work. It does not end at age eighty-five or ninety. You, my fair maiden, will live your purpose beyond the last breath you take. You are love.'

Four days after our talk she's calling me back. She is calling to tell me my visit with her was like a visit from above.

That's what keeps me trudging through my muck, cleaning up my own house so I can be of service to others.

TAKING IT SLOWER

If we do not shrink from honest self examination
we can never fail to accomplish the object our
hearts are set upon.

James Allen – As A Man Thinketh

TAKING it slow. Sometimes I hate slow. My personality wants it now. I get annoyed at my husband for taking so long to make his point. I hurry his words up, shorten the story, or ask him what's the point before he's finished talking. I'm rude. I need help.

Joe has taught me to slow down. It used to drive me crazy when we'd be in the car and I'd ask him what he thought and he'd answer, 'Nothing'. Nothing, I'd think to myself, I've already created two businesses, written the next chapter of my never completed novel in my mind, and figured out where we're going and what we're going to do when we get there; and Joe: 'nothing'.

As he'd continue driving thinking about nothing I'd roll my eyes and continue solving the world's problems in my head. Then he'd say, 'look over there' reaching across my face and pointing at an eagle. 'Do you see it landing in that tree?'

How can you see that? I'd think to myself. He mustn't be watching the road. I'd freak. Yet he was observing what I wasn't able to see. What else was I missing?

I realized he was so present as we drove that he observed everything. I, on the other hand, drove on autopilot, never quite knowing how I got somewhere but always arriving safe and sound. I started to think Joe might be on to something.

Driving was a perfect time to practice being in the present and observing everything around me. I practiced being Joe. I'd get into the car and tell myself we're going to think about nothing. I'd notice my hands on the steering wheel and foot on the gas or the brake. I started to notice the scenery and really see what was happening around me, not thinking about anything except what I was doing. Being mindful.

Joe continues to teach me. Everything I told myself I was good at, he was already doing. He was living in the present and I was pretending to. He was taking in everything and I was off somewhere in my mind missing life.

What are you thinking about?

Nothing. Good answer.

COINCIDENCES

When you live your life with an appreciation of coincidences and
their meanings,
you connect with the underlying field of infinite possibilities.

Deepak Chopra

6 'H ELLO young lady. I told you I'd make it and I
did.' The man standing in the doorway stood
as tall as a grizzly bear, his words were like
thunder breaking the silence.

He walked in and headed straight to the east corner of the
shop, his thin gray haired ponytail swayed in the rhythm
with his long strides. He walked in a circle around the
room. He took what seemed like no more than four giant
steps and in those brief moments seemed to have gathered
what he needed. He stood face to face with me at the
counter.

Under his arm he carried books, a bear claw hung from a
leather cord around his neck. He was wearing an old blue
tee shirt beneath an oversized leather jacket, and worn jeans.

A jacket sleeve was pushed up exposing a muscular arm
sprinkled with gray hair. I was sure he could pick up a log
and toss it just about anywhere he pleased.

'You don't remember me do you?' He asked.

My mind raced but I couldn't place him. Then it hit me.
The ferryboat ride two weeks before I opened Grandma's
Medicine Wheel, a resource center, in 1993.

51

I'll never forget that day. I was alone on the top deck in the very front of the boat where the wind blows so hard you have to yell to be heard. On this day I felt like I was the captain of the boat, standing at the helm leading this white stallion to port.

My cheeks were red and my hair was blowing in a chaotic whirlwind of delight. I leaned into the railing and raised my head to the sun. My eyes squinted from the brightness and I acknowledged my mom's presence, a ritual I started right after her death.

When the sun was out and shining it's brightest I felt Mom beside me. I felt as if she was telling me everything would be okay. I'd tell her I love her and imagine her telling me she loved me back. But that day was different. I kept talking into the salty air thanking her for the signs I believed she had sent me, signs that eventually led to me quitting my corporate career to open up Grandma's Medicine Wheel.

It was in the midst of my gratitude to Mom this big barrel of a man walked up and stood silently beside me looking out into the sound. It was as if someone had cued him, "*Okay now, walk out there. She's ready for you. It's time.*"

The moment got the best of me and any past inhibitions of talking to strangers were gone. I turned to him and, without waiting for a hello exchange, burst into my story. I told him about my journey since Mom died. My words tumbled out as fast as they could roll off my tongue.

I told this man about Mom dying and about the postcard that started the whole adventure. A postcard sent to my mother from a friend who didn't know she had died. I felt the postcard was meant for me, a message from Mom. It had an intriguing symbol on the front and the message written by the manufacturer of the card told the reader about the meaning of a circle.

I quoted the card, 'The Circle. In all Indian cultures you will find the image over and over again. You find it in the dances, in the art, and in the shape of lodging. But more than that the circle is the basis of American Indian beliefs. That everything is connected to everything else. All people and nature and the Maker, and no matter where you go and who you become you are still part of it all. And that cannot be ignored. Never.'

I shared with him about my son seeing the symbol on our living room ceiling and the other times the symbol seemed to be trying to tell me something. Eventually I found out it was a medicine wheel. Once I knew what the symbol was books about the medicine wheel practically fell off the shelves whenever I entered a bookstore. And pretty soon after more study and prayer it was clear what my next step would be.

I quit my job and in two weeks was opening up a resource center and bookstore called Grandma's Medicine Wheel.

I kept rambling. The sun was shining and the wind was on our faces. I felt alive for the first time in a long time and so this poor man was getting an earful.

I went on, 'I felt I was supposed to create a place where people could come and learn about the medicine wheel. Mom circled the wheel, eventually into the shadow of death. Now I was going to use what she went through physically, mentally, emotionally, spiritually, to create a safe place where people could embrace hope. I want to show them there are many ways to travel this road called Life.'

As the ferry was pulling in to the dock I invited him to the grand opening and concluded my stream of consciousness with maybe I'm nuts, but for once in my life I am living life from the heart.

He smiled with eyes that had not left mine, as if regardless of my non-stop chatter, whatever I said did mean something. Looking back I remembered the calmness, a genuine sharing of my joy, as if he knew something I had yet to discover. And when I handed him my card he told me in a gentle offhand voice that he knew a thing or two about the medicine wheel and he'd be in.

That was a year and a half ago and here he was standing in front of me.

54

'The ferry,' I said.

'Yes, the ferry,' he answered looking at me straight in the eyes. 'I told you'd I'd make it and here I am. Today was the day.'

I felt awkward. I didn't know what to say, recalling my bold behavior when we first met. 'I'm Sandy Powers,' I said unsure of myself. 'What can I do you for you?'

He put the books on the counter and said, 'I know who you are. My name is Roy Wilson. I am the shaman for the Cowlitz Tribe and a retired Methodist pastor of forty years. I am also the author of these books.'

My eyes went right to the one titled The Medicine Wheel. The embarrassment of our one-sided conversation was turning the pink in my cheeks a shade darker. I couldn't believe my nerve, telling him about the medicine wheel when he'd written a book on it. He saw my eyes and smiled, his calm demeanor once again quieting my apprehension.

'I have taught the Medicine Wheel for at least twenty years,' he said pausing before continuing, making sure my eyes held his. 'When I met you on the ferry, it wasn't a coincidence.'

Then he laughed as if we had shared a joke. I watched his face, not quite sure what to expect, and not quite sure what a shaman was. He went on to tell me how his father was Indian and his mother was non-Indian, that he'd been raised in both the white and the Indian world.

When he first became a preacher he led his church with only the white man's version of creation, but Father Sky eventually showed him his path was to bring both worlds together. He researched, studied, wrote books, and taught the Medicine Wheel around the country.

55

It was my turn to listen. I knew Roy being in my shop, meeting him as I did on the ferry was important. I was being gifted something by Life. Over the next few years he played an important role as my authentic self slowly emerged from a deep sleep.

Roy taught the medicine wheel teachings in our shop. He reached into our hearts to help bridge the Native teachings with those we find in the Bible and other cultures around the globe. He opened new worlds in order for us to live our lives more fully, to walk tall, and honor the gifts Father Sky gives each of us.

I learned that if you pay attention and listen, everything in life supports us, helping us make sense of where we've been, where we're at, and where we're going.

It has been many years since our meeting on the ferry. Grandma's Medicine Wheel is closed and I moved on living life from my heart. The lessons I received from Roy are a part of me forever and everyone I meet benefits because of him.

There are no chance meetings, no coincidences.

Everything happens for a reason.

SEPARATE
OR
CONNECTED

All things are bound together. All things connect.

Chief Sealth

QUANTUM physics, time, molecules, atoms, matter, all living all breathing. What was is, what is was, there is no division. Think a thought, is it really your thought or are you thinking a million other peoples thoughts?

I'm reminded again and again how connected we are despite our differences. It takes effort to appreciate and explore beyond our comfort zone. To look at differences through the eyes of our heart is a stretch. What are we afraid of, why do we stay in our comfortable box barely lifting the lid for air?

If someone acts out of ignorance, instead of creating a further division by bad-mouthing them, I try and remind myself to be thankful for my life. I recognize the courage it takes to love and not hate. Healthy boundaries are necessary but they are not an excuse to quit loving.

Why is it easy to hate? Why is it easy to bad-mouth? Why is it hard to love?

We are all in this world together. If only one belief is right or one race is right or one culture is right or one period in time right, why did Life create time and fill it with so much diversity?

Each person we meet offers us an opportunity to rub the sleep out of our eyes and wake up. Am I asleep? Is it time to wake up? What don't I see?

BIG BELLY LAUGHS

A day without laughter is a day wasted.

Charlie Chaplin

QUIT being so serious. 'Get out and laugh,' I hear in my head.

Rolling over to look at the clock I realize it's a dream. I close my eyes. My dead mother is talking to me. She's not actually talking to me, but she knows I can see her and hear her voice. I watch the movie in my mind unfold.

She's partying on a boat with some friends off the coast of France. She's telling me to quit being so serious and lighten up. I watch her on the boat and am amazed, but then again, not that amazed.

Of course Mom's heaven would have a ski boat in the water. Of course it would be summertime and she'd be doing her favorite things; soaking in the sun and laughing with friends. And of course she'd be wearing a way-too-tight bikini. I sense her wink at me acknowledging my observation as she sips her drink and goes back to her friends.

She's right. Lighten up. Take a break. Balance. Play. Take off your deep-sea diving helmet for a while and let loose.

'When was the last time you laughed big belly laughs?' I hear her ask as I watch her and her friends strip naked and jump off the boat. Get wild.

'Who needs a bathing suit?' I say to myself as I enter the dream. My modest self steps back as I feel my wild sensuous sexy side take over. Feel the cold water, splash, play, laugh, and enjoy the sun.

I'm frolicking in the water with everyone. Mom turns and winks at me splashing me in the face. 'Who cares', I tell myself, 'big is beautiful. Remember, I'm ageless. It doesn't matter that I've rarely worn a bathing suit let alone a bikini, it doesn't matter and you know why it doesn't matter, because clothes aren't an option.'

I hear myself giggle. In fact I break into big belly laughs.

Okay, Life, I hear you.

KNOW THY SELF

Make no mistake.
There is no sorrow in the universe that can extinguish your
persistent luminosity.

Wayne Muller- Legacy of the Heart

IT has been said by great spiritual leaders, one must root into one spiritual expression to go deep. What if one spiritual expression is not fertile ground for me? What if I was born to wander the vast richness of many cultures finding Truth everywhere? What if there is a richness that surpasses what could be found chained to one pew?

I cannot judge which road is right for each person. Who am I to judge? All I know is what is right for me.

I'm alive for a purpose much greater than the one I live. To live that purpose requires me to put both feet on the path. I must journey many miles into the kingdom Socrates named years ago, "Know Thy Self".

The entrance to the trail is overgrown with blackberry bushes. I've started down the path many times, but gave up long before reaching the lush land of wonder. They tell me that beyond the thorns and vines is a place where dark rich soil can be found and flowers grow dripping with sparkling jewels. I wasn't convinced it was true. I was far more content living in the kingdom everyone else coined, "I'm More Comfortable Here".

When my mother died in 1992 I found myself at the beginning of the trail, again. This time the kingdom "I'm More Comfortable Here" was destroyed. I had to go through the overgrown thickets with no tools but my bare hands.

After beating my way through overgrown blackberry bushes for what seemed like forever I came upon a small sign. 'This way to heaven.' Funny, how a little sign can give you strength. At the time Heaven sounded good. I didn't care if it was the heaven when you die or heaven on earth. Any heaven was better than where I was.

Those outside me were clueless to my inner chaos. Life goes on, people laugh, people cry, kids need feeding, husband needs loving, staff need assignments. Yet inside I was exhausted, battling my way through a war zone. The building blocks of my life had disintegrated. Life as I knew it was gone never to return again.

My immense love for my kids and my husband was my nourishment, along with bread, butter, and anything else deep fat fried. Okay, maybe an occasional chocolate bar or two. Remaining threads of my past blew in the wind snapping back and forth and hitting me hard. It took me several years to realize the transformational qualities those threads possessed. At the time they were too close for me to see.

Before long I came to a locked gate. There was no getting around it. On the ground was a piece of paper folded in two. I could tell there was something inside it. Carefully I unfolded the tattered page and found a key. Holding the key in my hand I read the words written on the paper. 'You are headed in the right direction, but to get there you must go through the kingdom of "The Past."

I unlocked the gate, not sure what to expect next.

ENTERING THE PAST

The potential power in everyone's life is
much greater than is now being realized.

Chief Roy Wilson, Cowlitz

STORIES filter from the past into the present when it's time. Nothing is recalled in gift boxes with lace and satin ribbons. Seconds of the past sometimes feel like years. It seems recall is broken up into fragments. Must be for a purpose.

When my foundation crumbled leaving nothing, the rebuilding process began. I could either rebuild unconsciously or rebuild with intention. This time I had a choice. I'd do it right. Even though I wanted it to happen now, it happens when it happens. Either accept it or fight it.

I know I'm here to serve the Creator. My first awareness of the Great Mystery came when I was eight years old. A woman gave me the Bible. She said, 'Read the red words, the words of Jesus.'

The red words showed up at the perfect time. Not much else made sense in my life. My parents were divorced and I was lost at sea in a dinghy. I was paddling around in tumultuous waters with no compass and no landmarks and feeling terribly alone. The red words calmed my panic and kept me from falling overboard.

A babysitter once tried to ease my suffering and said, 'Sandy, in ten years you'll look back on this period of your life and laugh.'

Laugh I never did, but look back, oh yes, time and time again. I didn't realize how deeply ingrained my younger years were, how they haunted me, and how they had formed me. My heart was ripped out of me and thrown behind a fortress built by a powerful beast. There was a door in the wall, but no key. The beast ate it, for my protection.

Was I the beast?

I am not proud of the things I did to survive pain.

In my heart's place came a version of the Master Manipulator and Chief Guilt Slinger I'd witnessed far too many times as a child. I was a fierce warrior able to battle the strongest of giants and crush them with a single glance.

Can one person be so loving and so mean at the same time? I could. I was. Without realizing it I left victims along side the road, justifying every action or inaction or reaction I made.

Wake up. 'Wake up', my true nature echoed from behind the fortress, 'wake up.'

Mahatma Gandhi said, 'happiness is when what you think, what you say, and what you do are in harmony.' I was not in harmony. I was all over the map. I was everything at once. Loving, bitchy, mean, kind, caring, snappy, and reactive. I was on guard and in control. As long as my hand was in it or on it, life was okay.

To be fair I was a really, really good mother. I made a vow when I got pregnant that my children would never doubt they were loved. They would know my love for them would and could move the Earth. Period.

My love ran deep, streaming from a bottomless pool reserved only for my kids. Their love tethered me to the earth. Regardless of my inward or outward battles, I never gave in to the demons that almost got me before my children entered my life.

My youngest son, a wise old soul I'm sure, used to write poetry as a kid. There is a calm about him. On the day of his birth it was as if he were sent to tell me it's time to wake up, I'm here, it will all be okay.

I'll never forget those next couple of snowy January days. No one ventured to the hospital to see us because of the weather. When his dad went home to take care of his siblings we were left alone. When he looked at me, there was nowhere to hide. He could and always has been able to see me even when I couldn't see myself.

I didn't think anyone knew the real me, but my children have always known me for who I am.

Back then adults in my life usually ended up hurting me and if I had a chance I'd hurt them back. If they'd reject me or say something to lose my trust out would come my fangs and stinger and claws. Their actions were an attack. And as an adult I could chew them up, spit them out, and move on without them ever knowing what hit.

One afternoon I came home from work and headed to my room. Half way down the stairs I heard the voice of Joe, my second husband, the love of my life, talking with his mother on the phone. 'Mom, I'm going to leave this weekend. Ever since her mom died nothing I do is right. She keeps telling me to leave and I don't know what else to do.'

I couldn't believe what I was hearing. Yes, I had told him to leave, many times, but now he was really going.

65

My theory had been that one day he'd leave anyway so why prolong the inevitable, better me to initiate rejection than be rejected.

Since Mom died my ability to hold back emotions ceased, they were being shot as lethal bullets from every pore of my body. Crying one minute, snappy the next, nothing after that, the perpetual cycle of craziness was so strong and I was so weak. I often gave in to my insanity. I'd see people laughing while driving in their cars and all I wanted to do was scream at them, 'Stop laughing, my God, don't you know my mother's dead?' But they didn't, life went on.

Hearing my husband crying, telling his mom he was giving up because that's what I wanted jolted me. This was a man who showered me with more love than any other adult had in a long, long time. He was the one trying with all his might in every way he knew how to comfort me through my grieving process and all I kept doing was asking him to leave. Why?

When he hung up the phone I ran into the room. He was wiping his eyes and startled to see me. I dropped to my knees and before he could say a word I begged, 'Please don't go. I promise, I promise I will get help. I will do anything I have to do to heal myself. I don't want to lose you. Please forgive me. Please don't leave. I didn't mean it. I'm sorry.'

Why did saying I'm sorry take so much out of me? Was I that weak, had I fooled myself all those years into thinking it took more courage and strength to shove someone out of my life? Did I have everything backwards? What was wrong with me?

He opened his arms and I fell into them. With his warmth wrapped around me I buried my head in his chest. We both cried. At that moment I knew I would heal. I would not be a victim any longer. How I would accomplish that I had not a clue. It didn't matter. I wasn't going to lose him. I'd do it.

COMMITMENT TO HEAL

"Commitment is what transforms a promise into a reality"

Abraham Lincoln

ROLL up my sleeves and get busy, heal. Get it done so I can start life.

Wrong.

Healing is a life-long process. Once I'm done I end up doing it again and again until all the triggers are gone. Pain fights for our attention any way it can. It doesn't stop until peace prevails and love is more visible than not.

Buttons being pushed means more to heal. How many buttons do I have? How many buttons are in a button factory?

When I started healing, parts of me were afraid to come out. I'd beaten them up pretty bad over the years. Constantly berating the weakest parts of me was such an ingrained habit I didn't know I was doing it. The consummate critic had free rein and loomed large. What was left of me didn't think I was strong enough to handle this cold cruel world and wanted to keep me under wraps. Who was I, Sybil?

Throughout several years I licked wounds, nurtured myself, and explored my past with new lenses.

In fact sometimes I was sick of healing or thought I was done healing and I'd tell myself, 'Okay, time to wrap up this heal fest. We're healed. Done deal. End of story.' Before long I could hear the still small voice asking me, 'are you sure you are healed?' Yes. I'd snap back. I'm done.

I learned fast that snapping back is not the wisest choice unless you like lying on broken glass while someone jumps on your tummy. I take more time now. I spend time with myself reflecting and contemplating. I want to make sure I really believe I've loved myself enough, tackled what I need to tackle before giving the nod, yes.

Why? Because when I give the yes nod Life tests my opinion. In the beginning I got to rest before the test hit. But the more I healed the stronger I got. Life knew it. I'd let my guard down and get comfortable and without fail a test would come proving me wrong. On the other hand, the further into healing I got the more tests I did pass and the more rejoicing occurred. Triggers do evaporate and, in their place, peace settles in.

Dipping into a like situation is the ultimate test. When all my senses are exposed to a similar situation I scan my body and ask myself, are there any more triggers? Then I scan my emotions and do the same thing. If I experience peace, I know I've healed.

All parts of me are connected. I like that. It makes sense. If I work on one part all the other parts benefit. The healer I choose is secondary to the responsibility I must take to heal. I can't dump the healing responsibility on to anybody. I use the technical talents of highly trained professionals if needed, but the main component consists of rolling up my sleeves and becoming aware of my attitude. I must be willing to go the extra mile and reach deep inside of myself to touch the tender parts of me. By nurturing and loving myself, and being patient with my progress, quality of life blossoms.

Healing is about finding a genuine sense of well being.

70

Each time I heal I experience peace. My wounded part is free to fly as a peaceful memory. Instead of my wounds showing up in my attitude, or manifesting into a physical symptom, we both rest.

Learning to set myself free happened bit by bit.

Licking my wounds was the first step. Loving myself was harder. I liked parts of me. I've always had yummy lips, great eyes. I'm a good mom. But I hated other parts of me. My dark ugly side I tried to silence, stuff in a cement block and throw out to sea, yet she'd always wash up on shore and find an air hole somewhere and scream louder than ever.

I learned that when she tries to get my attention to let her be, quit trying to silence her. She's part of me. She has a voice and wants to be heard. She was stuffed, stabbed, and tortured for far too long. Whenever she escapes the prison I put her in she blurts out in not so appropriate language or behavior faster than a speeding bullet. She's never sure where or when she'll be captured and locked up again. There is no time for polite etiquette. She voices herself in whatever she can to get my attention. Over the years I've come to recognize her tribal call. It's not pretty but I've slowly learned to listen and give her a voice.

Finally I 'get' the ugly part of me is expressing herself in the only way she can. She's coming out of the wild with no skills. She's raw and real. It's up to me to listen with my heart and not judge her approach. It's important to take the time to ask her why she's here and not shut her up or minimize her complaint. I've learned to listen conveying we'll do whatever it takes to heal. We're worth it. I've learned to love even the yucky parts of myself.

71

Solo gigs suck. 'I can do it alone. I don't need anyone' was my mantra for far too long. No more. I ask for help and allow people in to a place where things aren't tied up in neat tidy packages, a place where vulnerability hangs out and makes a mess. That part of me doesn't possess my usual wit and charm. She is raw and clumsy, bared for the world to see.

It's taken far more courage to be real than it ever did to stay mired in the gunk of my unhealthy habits. No longer will I allow myself to dine on dysfunction and pretend to know all the answers.

Freedom required getting raw and real. For a control freak I was sure that meant instant death.

I was wrong.

WEIGHT

You have to stay in shape. My grandmother, she started walking
five miles a day when she was 60. She's 97 today and we don't
know where the hell she is.

Ellen Degeneres

NEGLECTING what can be changed is nuts, or is it?
My weight for instance, why do I put off losing the
weight? Why do I let myself stay the same? Is it
that the effort doesn't seem to add up to the benefit? Am I too
lazy?

I can easily sweet talk myself into anything. I don't think I
look as awful as others may think. I feel healthy. I work out.
Yet, I feel better when I start losing the pounds. I keep
myself looking the best I can with the weight I have. Clean,
nice clothes, makeup on, hair kept in style.

Yet something bothers me. I think weird thoughts like, oh
God, what if I get sick and have a heart attack or stroke and
someone has to lift my body out of my bedroom and carry it
down the stairs? What if they couldn't? What if they had to
hire a crane and break a wall down? What if the news
channels came and aired the whole embarrassing
experience? Yikes.

I panic thinking of the burden I will place on Joe or my
kids. But those thoughts ebb away only to be revived later,
after a big bite of a juicy cheeseburger. Cyclical thoughts,

never staying too long, but feeling shame or guilt because of my choices and the burden it may place on others.

I once heard an interview with a famous singer who was also overweight. She said, 'I never think I'm that fat until I see a picture of myself.' Me too. Some people think of themselves as fat and ugly. I don't, neither did she. I'd never heard that thought said out loud before. Even I could see she was getting big. But she didn't see it. She created a fantasy in her own mind that she looked good. I guess I do too.

When I look in the mirror, some days I love what I see and other days I don't. My prayer is that I take my weight off and do something once and for all before it's too late. Like many other overweight folks I could write the books on nutrition. It isn't that I lack the knowledge; it's that I lack the discipline. Immediate gratification wins. There's more to the story I'm sure.

How can I be so disciplined and dedicated to being the best I can be, but ignore this part of my life? What's wrong with me?

I am a work in progress.

HEROES

Without heroes, we are all plain people, and
don't know how far we can go.

Bernard Malamud

MY cousin was hit with an aggressive form of
cancer, non-Hodgkin's lymphoma, a disease
with a life of its own. I was mad and sad,
frustrated about his cancer. He'd listen to me vent and then
he'd come up with these gems teaching me more about life.

After his diagnosis he said, 'It isn't so much the disease
that gets you, it's your mind. It tries to take your time and
energy. It crams you full of worry. My body doesn't feel bad,
but my mind doesn't care. I was going to go out last
weekend, but all I could do was sit on the couch.'

Any estrangement he had with family or friends vanished
when he was diagnosed. He said, 'There comes a time when
you have to let it go. Life is too short. It's hurting nobody
but me. I don't have time to waste.'

Whenever I'd start talking negative about someone or
something, he'd come back with a little laugh and say, 'Now
ain't we perfect'. He wouldn't tell me to shut up, instead his
quip would remind me not to waste time or the energy
getting angry, it makes no sense.

He was right. We'd finish talking and I'd hang up the
phone wondering who was this great sage? My cousin Mike
is one of my heroes.

Another hero of mine is Joe's sister Kelli, my sister-in-love. When she was diagnosed with breast cancer she jumped into warrior woman mode.

Despite her fears she said, 'I hope I'm taking on the demon for the rest of our family. I don't want anyone to go through what I'm going through'. She lost a breast, her hair, and her health, and for a long time she was sore and emotionally wrung out, but she kept on fighting. She kept reaching out, asking for a lifeline. She wasn't afraid to ask for what she needed.

She survived. Several months later when her back was hurting and her worst fears were swirling in her mind, she had to go in for a bone scan. She remembered a book she'd had for a few months. It was on forgiveness.

The morning after the bone scan she opened the book for the first time and read seventy-five pages. She called me, excited. She could barely get her words out. I could hear a shift in her voice.

She was looking forward to a gathering later on that day to practice what she had learned. She wanted to experience the love she was feeling with the individuals that were normally hard to be around. She concluded our conversation saying, 'My cancer was perfect'.

Wow. I don't know if I could say my cancer was perfect. What did that mean? I wasn't sure, but what I did know was that a blockage deep within her emotional body was gone. She was free flowing in the land of the healed. I knew everything was divinely perfect.

Her test came back negative for bone cancer. Her back was a mess, but the breast cancer had not metastasized. She'd worked through something at the deepest level of her being. She'd been working hard to heal meditating and being in gratitude in addition to other traditional and not so traditional treatments. Because of her hard work the contents of the book resonated with her heart. Her anger, pain, and frustration were nurtured into wholeness.

We can give credit to a doctor, a book, a spiritual teacher, really to anything for healing, but the bottom line is everything before us is a tool if we choose to use it. My heart can transform, as can Kelli's. We are the ones who must take the ingredients in to the heart and allow ourselves to be transformed from this to that, from here to there.

We possess everything we need to experience the happiness we seek.

If meditation washes the mind, gratitude cleanses the heart.

Why don't we do it more often? What excuse could we possibly have?

VALUE

Strive not to be a success, but rather to be of value.

Albert Einstein.

VALUE. Valuing myself. Valuing others. What does being of value look like?

When I feel valued and appreciated my defenses go down. I sink back into the calm. I love more. My compassion reaches further. Small things don't irritate me as fast. I give more freely. Laughter and joy pour from me.

Am I of value when I value others? What does value look like?

What happens when our children, our co-workers, our friends, our bosses feel valued? Is it possible to be of value to our enemies? Am I creative enough to find a thread of value to appreciate when value seems to have vanished?

Every day my intention is the same, to be of value. I want to add to this world in a positive way. I want to make sure whatever I say or do adds to my life and to the lives of those around me.

Standing in the raining waters of Value my apprecia-tion for life forms a rainbow and my commitment to love shines.

DAILY LIVING

We must always remember that the path
does not produce the change; it only places us
where the change can occur.

Richard J. Foster – Celebration of Discipline

I'M learning to live with daily doses of doubt. I proclaim my Faith every day. Life is a gift. I am humbled by the miracles happening in my life, the coincidences, the chance meetings, the 'aha' moments. I believe more today than I did the day before.

Even though my faith is unshakable, doubt is never far away.

When doubt and fear climb into my bed and start moving up the sheets to sit on my chest I never allow them to win. I am far greater than my emotions.

It is only the hectic pace of daily living that nips at my feet. I must get quiet, reconnect, clear my mind, and remember what I know. There is nothing greater, stronger, or more powerful than the Love of the Great Mystery.

Doubt is part of my daily living, but I have the means to eliminate it; Love.

GRIEF

Even a happy life cannot be without a
measure of darkness.

Carl Jung

W HEN my mother died, my heart broke and no one
could fix me and I couldn't fix myself. Grief lived
my life for me while I was lost in the desert.
Working with others lost in the desert I've heard the same cries. In
our own way and in our own time we come back to the living. We
come back, not the same, but different. Hear the voice of my pain.

I have to believe Truth resides in me.

But if that's true, why do I feel like a living ghost? Why do
I feel naked and exposed with nowhere to hide? Why do I
want to scream? Why does no one hear my pain? Why did
this happen? Why can't I think? Why do I feel guilty? When
will the pain go away?

Don't take my pain. What will be in its place? Will I forget,
or minimize, or belittle the monumental love I had and lost?
Please don't take my pain away. It is all I have left.

Keep me in limbo land so I never have to feel again. Why
am I alive? What is the point?

'Keep asking questions,' I hear my heart say.

Questions. 'Damn you,' I scream at the top of my lungs.
'You are supposed to love me.'

I'm not living and I'm not dead.

Is this love?

CHANGE

*Everything in the future will improve if you are
making a spiritual effort now.*

Paramhansa Yogananda – The Essence of Self-Realization

I'D like to yell 'stop' at change. Please, for one moment let me catch my breath. But change has no ears.

It's like love. Love isn't something you bargain with. It's something you choose to participate in. It's a freight train moving nonstop. Either have the courage to hop on board or don't.

Do I have the courage to participate in change? It's easier to bury my head and let life happen. Or is it?

Change happens with us or without us. I choose to participate in change. I choose to create the change I desire.

Sometimes life just happens, but sometimes we can make life happen. Both are change.

Catch your breath and hop on board.

SPIRITUAL PRACTICE

We can learn about the spiritual experiences
of others, or we can bring meaningful practice
into our own daily lives.

Rabbi David A. Cooper – God Is A Verb

MY spiritual practice is first and foremost in my life. I need it. My sanity depends on it. The intimacy I have with my family and friends exists because of it. My Faith goes beyond what I can control. Faith anchors me. Everything I am comes from that.

When life is sane I dive deeper into my studies and my practices, because in an instant life can be insane. Life hits hard. There is something greater than ourselves that determines when the earth will quake.

Paying attention to the still small voice helps me navigate life. In order to pay attention I do what it takes to listen. That is why I search, gathering wisdom from every port.

The sooner I hear the still small voice the faster I can take action. Ignoring that inner nudging only leads to greater hits. Hit me once okay, but hit me twice... wake up.

FAITH

Now faith is the assurance of the things we hope for, being the
proof of the things we do not see and
the conviction of their reality.

Hebrews 11:1

EVERY few years an internal alarm clock goes off and
it's time to reinvent myself. Even though I don't
know what I'm going to do I get excited and scared. I
don't know what this new life will look like, but I know it
will be good.

I love that I'm willing to take action. When I recognize an
inner urging I chew on it with my heart to determine my
next move. Internal alarm clocks don't come with
guidebooks. Instead, I must take my inkling, turn it into a
goal, and rely on my mind and heart to create the course of
action. The outcome from each step I take determines the
next move. If going down one road doesn't pan out I head
down a different road.

A door slamming in my face doesn't take the wind out of
me nearly as much as it used to. Doors either open or close.
If one closes I move to the next door.

In my youth I'd pound on a closed door until my knuckles
bled. I'd crumble to the ground exhausted when I couldn't
get in. I was sure I had failed. I'd convince myself the only
way to go was through that door.

Didn't I believe I was being guided? Was I so off base? How could I trust myself again? I'd ask, slinking back to my comfort zone.

Over the years I matured and my faith grew. I wondered if other doors existed. What if an open or closed door were the guidepost for my next move? What if I used the eyes of my heart to find another door?

Other doors exist, they always have. It takes effort to pull away from a closed door and hit the trail. No matter how much I wanted a fairy to show up and take my hand, it didn't happen. There's no white rabbit to follow, there's only me, and the Great Mystery. When one door closes I'm shown another door. There's always another door.

When I step into the unknown and trust each step, my goal becomes a reality.

INTUITION

The intuitive mind is a sacred gift and the
rational mind is a faithful servant.
We have created a society that honors the
servant and has forgotten the gift.

Albert Einstein

INTUITION, could it be the language of the heart?
Every culture tells stories about someone receiving
visions and direction from the Great Mystery, guidance
from dreams or signs. Hasn't the course of history been
altered by visions?

My role in life is to foster spiritual growth. In order to do
that I must diligently clean my own house, listen with the
ears and see with the eyes of my heart. I don't put all my
eggs in the intuitive basket and toss everything else out. I
must take it a step further and listen. Taking whatever I
think I see or hear and visiting the sacred in heart.

Marsha Sinetar says, 'anyone who intuits our life's
essential vision or themes and some how affirms these
so that we reach out for them is an artist, an artist of
encouragement'.

What if I'm an artist of encouragement? In order to fulfill
that role I need to be still. Instead of jabbering away asking
for this and that, I must take the time to listen. Listen in the
stillness.

Learning about the symbolism used by different cultures
is like discovering another language. It is another way for

91

me to focus in with God. By understanding the different meanings of symbols more possibilities present themselves revealing other doors to walk through and explore. Heightened awareness coupled with expanded knowledge of what symbols mean, are essential to living my life fully.

They say non-verbal communication is the most potent form of communication.

Does that apply to hearing the Great Mystery speak to us? If it does, am I willing to stretch and learn a new language? And if not, why not? Am I too scared?

Why do the words *sacred* and *scared* possess the same letters? Does that mean anything?

SILENCE

In the attitude of silence the soul finds the path in a clearer light, and what is elusive and deceptive resolves itself into crystal clearness.

Mahatma Gandhi

HOW come we have time to worry, but we don't have time to be quiet? Is it because we don't believe getting quiet will really, really, help? Or do we have too many other important things to do, like watch T.V.?

I wrestle with a big tiger throughout the day. He thinks that filling my day with busyness is the best thing for me and I fight for silence. Way too often he wins.

My Heart doesn't yell like my noisy mind. The mind works on getting my attention any way it can. When the mind and heart finally unite the harmony is heaven, but that takes practice.

In the beginning the mind put up mega resistance. But, thankfully, the Heart is patient. She waits for me with open arms. She knows I'll be back. She loves me, warts and all.

CONFIDENCE

Directed faith makes every thought crackle with power.

Napoleon Hill – Think and Grow Rich

MY nephew came to live with us several years ago and he stayed through high school. It was a blessing having his presence in my life, but it didn't start out that way.

Anger and rage bottled for so long in someone is bound to come out and it did. I'd been told from the start he'd fail, he was bad news, that eventually something was going to go terribly wrong, he'd end up doing something unthinkable, or worse. He was kicked out of a wilderness school and had nowhere to go. His mother had no more options. His father lived out of state with a long list of his own personal problems and never offered to take him.

I could only imagine how my nephew felt about himself. We'd been separated since he was five years old. But with one phone call from my sister asking if I'd take David our lives changed.

Most of my adult life I've worked on being the best I can be. Reading, studying, gathering tools for life is second nature. Putting those tools into practice is another story. When life tells me it's time to come out and play with the big boys, my tummy immediately does flip-flops.

Am I ready to live what I believe I know?

Having David move in was a given. When my mother died she made me promise I'd keep the family together. On her deathbed she added 'please take care of David, he needs you'. Little did I know how true that would turn out to be.

My sister who is ten years younger, my brother, and I were loved, but we experienced it doubting love's depth until much later in our lives.

When I was young I didn't know how to shut up, or not shake the boat. I would tell it like I saw it. My little brother used to ask, 'Why do you have to say anything, it only makes it worse.' He was right, but I knew even as a child we deserved more. We deserved to be cared for, loved consistently, and nurtured, even though the adults in our lives were too caught up in their own problems to recognize our pain.

This book isn't about making anyone a bad guy, because at some point we all end up being the bad guy to someone, somewhere, sometime. It's about healing, moving on and finding the happiness we deserve.

When my nephew called me from the wilderness school, he was at his lowest point. We all know they send the bad kids to this type of school and now he was being kicked out. When he asked if he could come live with me I said yes. His voice, barely audible, replied, 'You really want me'. Yes I want you.

I'd been told the worst about this kid, but my heart kept telling me that underneath the worst of us, we are all the same. We have God stuff in us. That would be my focus. Not on his past errors, but his potential, his greatness, his unlimited pool of love. He didn't know he had it, but I did. And the only way to show him his was to model mine. Was I up to it?

It's easy to be loving and kind when things are going good, but when everything hits the fan you find out what you're really made of.

I kept thinking about Mahatma Gandhi, his life was his message.

Joe wasn't thrilled when I crawled into bed in the darkened room and asked, 'Honey, is it okay if David comes to live with us?'

There was no answer. We'd been together thirteen years. He'd been waiting to have me to himself since we wed. He was my second husband and he knew my children were top priority in my life. When they graduated from high school and went off to college to live their own lives, he thought at last it's us, alone.

Wrong. A young girl battling with drugs and alcohol moved in and stayed for a year and a half. That period was also filled with modeling love. Love didn't mean being a mushball and letting people walk all over me. Love meant checking in with my heart and making sure what I'm doing is coming from that deep place within and not some half-cocked emotion I haven't dealt with. It's having strong boundaries and doing what's right even when others won't like me.

Eventually she reconciled with her father and moved back home.

Two weeks after she moved out my sister called about David.

'How can we say no?' Joe said into the darkness of our room. We were both staring at the ceiling. He continued, 'You made a promise to your mom you'd take care of David, you'd be there for him. I was there. How can we say no?'

I rolled over and hugged him. I am so blessed to have a man who loves me so much. He knew I had to. There was no question. David was coming home.

People have said, 'Oh, you did so much for him', and to that I reply it was a tag team. We provided a space for David to bring out his emotions and work with them, to heal himself, to find out what an incredible guy he really is. He did the work. It was his choice.

We both grew.

There isn't anyone I know who is capable of healing someone else. We can provide an environment that encourages and supports healing, but the individual must do the work. David did the work.

It took everything I had in me to take responsibility for my actions. When I snapped at him or yelled or was impatient, I had to step back and reconnect with my heart to remember the big forest picture and not get stuck in the trees. My goal was to remember that we were both much greater than what was going on at the time.

He saw me get upset, deal with it, and love him consistently. He learned how to deal with different moods and I learned how to walk my talk.

I told him how much I believed in him, because I do. I believe in every person alive. I believe we each have transformational qualities and can turn our lives around if we choose. That is one of my strongest beliefs.

I couldn't turn his life around. He had to, and he did.

He came to us at age fifteen. He brought with him zero credits from his first year of high school as a ninth grader. At the end of two and a half years he graduated with all As and Bs. He graduated on time, taking two correspondence courses to catch up on his credits. He learned about friendship. He learned when someone has a bad day and takes it out on you, it really isn't about you; it's about them. He learned so much and so did I.

His graduation was a miracle. What a tag team we were. He moved to California to live with his grandparents and go to college. He is thriving. He likes himself. He has confidence and it shows.

Confidence allows us to be who we really are, a loving and kind and calm presence in others' lives. There's a big difference between being cocky and having confidence. It seems whenever my ego gets out of hand, life has a way of bringing me down a notch or two. Something happens and I fall to my knees and I remember how much I still have to learn.

Being humble and having confidence are a great marriage. The two together create harmony.

RISKING

We must journey to find the life we prize.

John Eldredge – The Journey of Desire

OR several years whenever a special friend was having a birthday I would venture to the beach in search of a treasure. Turning off the engine of my car I'd close my eyes and ask Life to lead me to this special present. Then I'd walk down the path and begin my search.

Without fail I'd end up finding a moon shell, those glorious white shells with large openings, natural magnets for my ears. I'd imagine wise women from long ago whispering the secrets of all time, their wisdom somehow encoded in the swirling echoing noise.

A gift from the sea was always mine to give. I'd write a heartfelt note and tuck it into this special prize.

Yet, never in all my times of doing this had I taken a shell for myself.

One Saturday morning my husband Joe asked if I wanted to go down to the beach with our black Lab Lucy. Sitting in the car I thought I'd sure like to find a moon shell just for me. As soon as I said the words guilt washed over me. Was I nuts? Finding moon shells was about my friends, not me. I was lucky enough to find one for them let alone finding one for me. I wanted one for no special purpose other than my own desire, but I couldn't keep the thought from rolling over and crushing every objection.

101

Before we got out of the car I set my intention for the trip. Life, please find me a moon shell. Please, one for me? I'd really, really like a moon shell, just for me.

Joe was clueless to the dialogue I was having with Life as we walked hand in hand to cross the overpass down to the beach.

When we reached the driftwood, rocks, and sand, Lucy and my husband went off to find their own treasures. I trailed behind, which was my normal MO, and kept my eyes peeled for my present.

Soon, out of the corner of my eye, I saw a tide pool. It was partially hidden under a large tree trunk washed up on shore what looked like eons ago. The water was murky. An old kelp ball was laying half in and half out. Lo and behold, a moon shell was peeking its crown out of the murk, a dirty broken moon shell.

It was the ugliest moon shell I'd ever seen. In my book it was an automatic reject, not a keeper I'd tell my kids when they asked holding up a tiny broken piece of a shell, or dirty feather in my direction.

I held it out at arm's length. Not only was the water not fit for a jellyfish, it smelled as if it had traveled around the world a few times inside the belly of a whale.

But then I thought, how ungrateful you are. You asked for a moon shell and you got one. How picky can you get? Do you know how rare it is to find even one moon shell on this beach?

Holding my breath I looked at the shell again. If I took it home, put it in bleach, maybe it would clean up okay. But it was broken, it too had rolled in the belly of a whale hitting every tooth that big guy had.

102

Then put it back.

I heard the still small voice inside say.

But I can't, I mean, it is a shell.

I asked for one, so I should keep it.

Then keep it.

But I don't like it. It's ugly.

Then put it back.

But what if I don't find another one.

Then keep it.

But it's ugly.

Then put it down.

The dialogue continued. I looked down the beach for my husband. He was getting smaller and smaller.

OK, I'll put it down. My body bent over ready to set it down ever so carefully in a spot I was sure I'd remember just in case.

No, I can't do that, that's cheating. If I don't want it, let it go, I told myself, actually put it down and don't look back.

I did. It took everything I had not to turn around and try to memorize where I'd placed that wretched thing in the event I'd change my mind on the way back.

Then I caught myself. Even though I had put the shell down I was still consumed with it, my thoughts were possessed. I'd taken several steps not even realizing what was in front of me.

I stopped and looked up at the sun. Then I said into the air, 'I am letting go of the shell. I deserve a nice, white, not broken moon shell and even if I never find one I'm not settling for less.'

I closed my eyes and held my head up toward the sun feeling its warmth on my cheeks for the first time that day. I opened my eyes and noticed how blue the sky was. I felt my feet in the sand, how my shoes sunk in as I walked. I felt a slight breeze off the water and noticed how the rocks glistened when wet. I kept walking toward Joe.

I was noticing everything, a little feather, wisps of beach grass poking though the sand and even a little rock crab in another clear tide pool. I looked out in the shallow water and there it was, a moon shell, a big, white, beautiful moon shell.

I shouted out into the sea air, 'Thank you, Life, thank you so much.' Then I noticed out of the corner of my eye another moon shell, another big, beautiful white moon shell. I picked it up too and waved to my husband calling, 'Look, look at all these moon shells.'

He ran back and we were both picking up shells and putting them into our pockets. I was giggling, laughing, my feet soaking wet, my pockets full of sand and shells.

When we got to the car we took out the shells. There were thirteen big, beautiful, white moon shells. All the way home I gave thanks and smiled to myself. Tears tasted salty as I licked them off my cheeks. I couldn't believe it. I was holding thirteen moon shells in my lap. How blessed was I?

It is now several years later and those beautiful moon shells have a home in a basket that sits in a bay window soaking up the sun. A basket that travels with me and sits in the center of any circle I have been privileged to facilitate. To this day they continue to tell a story to remind me not to settle for less, to listen, to believe, to let go, and to live.

MEDITATION

The cave you enter holds the treasure you seek.

Joseph Campbell

THE cave I entered was my heart; the treasure I found was me.

There once was a wise Buddhist monk named Luang Phaw Wat Paknam. Teaching meditation became his life's purpose. Though born curious, he took care of his family duties while seeking answers to life's questions. When no more could be gathered from outside sources he went inward and his world expanded. He developed a method of meditation. It became his life mission to pass the method on to others.

He knew how busy the mind gets, always straying here and there, never happy to stop. He gave the mind duties to perform, a mantra, words to say, and something to picture, a visualization, all while training it to be quiet. He knew that was the quickest way to train the mind; give it something to do. When he did, his method brought tremendous success.

If you continued to practice his technique, eventually the mantra or visualization was not needed. Your mind was trained to enter stillness with ease. He suggests we must train ourselves to stop running heedlessly from here to there. When we do not allow our mind to boss us around from thought to thought our lives change in remarkable ways.

One of his followers is a former Buddhist monk who, with his wife, now owns our local Thai restaurant. They shared a teaching with me, 'as we wash our body we need to wash our mind. Wash your mind like you brush your teeth. No expectation for the mind, but to clean it.'

Another tradition from the East says 'when you give gratitude in your life you are washing your heart. Washing your heart and cleansing it helps you reconnect to the kingdom of heaven within'. That is the place Jesus spoke about.

Going inward and being quiet is my goal. Turning off the radio and TV. Being comfortable with time, being quiet even though I get bored. Being quiet even though thoughts dart in and out.

What I get from stillness is peace. I am cleansed and start anew, connected to God in a profound way which helps me in every area of my life. Meditation directs me back into the calm, a place of divine contentment. The place where I try to live my life, the place I want to be in when it's my time to go.

Meditation soothes me, if I choose to let it.

FORGIVENESS

If you are afraid to open to love, it is only because
you're so very tender.

Stephen C. Paul – In Love

TENDER. Am I tender? When I think about this
person or that one, does a sense of anger, sorrow, or
frustration fester below the surface or jump into my
mind unannounced and make me want to run?

Where I'm tender I nurture myself. Learning to listen and
give voice to my pain is a priority. When I do I'm free to cut
the shackle of pain by forgiving. Sometimes I think I've
forgiven, but the body never lies. That's why I listen.

Many books are written about forgiveness and many
counselors are capable of helping one through the steps.
Despite all the tools, I wrestled with forgiveness for thirty
years.

One day it was time. I found the courage to forgive. In
return the gates of love opened, and the love my dad had
been trying to give me flooded in.

Why did I block out his love? Why couldn't I get over it?
I'd been agonizing for years.

I love my dad more than anything, but felt that he failed
loving me when I needed him the most. When I was doing
my healing work and needed him to hear my pain, and
blame and anger and anguish, he listened with an open
heart. Yet I continued to shut him out. Was I taking revenge?
And if so, who was I hurting?

How long does one have to suffer before the score is even? Is it ever even? Who is the judge?

My father is the kindest, gentlest soul I know. His eyes speak a million words. He wears his heart on his sleeve. Because of choices he made long ago I held him prisoner and it tortured both of us.

One day he wrote me a poem and faxed it to me. He said I was his firstborn. He said if he could go back in time and change things he would, but he couldn't. He asked me when or if I would ever be able to let go.

I'll never forget that day. Tears ran down my cheeks as I pulled the fax from the machine and read the poem again, and again. There were no words to say what I felt. The awareness of my behavior hit me straight on, showing me how mean I was to him. How twisted my behavior could be.

As if hurting him was going to bring back what I lost. It never could. Time moved on, but I hadn't. The choice either to start loving him fully and allowing him to love me was now or I was going to continue this insane game. The choice was mine.

Everything I wanted was in front of me. All I had to do was forgive him and ask for him to forgive me. I told myself I'd forgiven him, but my behavior didn't match my words.

It was really hard to call him and admit I'd been a schmuck. I'd thrown my scorpion tail around too many times. Arsenic lost its potency against one word uttered out of my mouth. One look from me would have anyone down for the count. I had all the moves covered. If someone hurts me, watch out. I'm not a kid anymore, I'm lethal.

When my daughter was in high school and had a track meet at a school nearby I called Dad and asked if he'd like to go, then I threw in, if he could find the time. He said yes, he'd be there.

After the meet we were walking alone on our way back to the car. He said, 'When you asked me if I wanted to attend the meet you made it sound like you didn't think I would take the time to see my granddaughter.' I joked his comment off laughing, 'oh Dad you know I was just joking'. 'Okay hon', he said. We both said good-bye and got into separate cars.

When I put on my seatbelt I sat there. He was right. I did hurt him. When I thought about my invitation with the trailer... if he could find the time... He was right. I was guilt tripping him for past choices, still. I was pathetic. I was almost forty years old and I was still acting like a hurt child.

I looked at myself in the rearview mirror and said, 'Next time you see Dad you are going to tell him he was right and ask for his forgiveness.' On my way back to work I went to the bank and as I was walking in, guess who was walking out?

Dad. My stomach was immediately in knots. He was headed down the walk and I was headed up. I had only a few seconds either to back out or speak up.

"Oh, hi honey," he said surprised to see me.

"Hi Dad," I answered wanting to walk past him and into the bank, but I stopped. "Dad, can I talk to you for a minute?"

"Sure, babe. What's up?"

"You were right," I blurted out. "I'm sorry. I did mean to hurt you. Will you forgive me?"

His eyes twinkled, "Yes. No problem, dear."

In an instant it was over. All the years of not feeling love vanished. I loved my dad and he loved me. He held the bank door open for me and we said goodbye, our lives never to be the same again.

It was a curious event I've thought about several times. All the years I wasted shackled in my pain. All I had to do was forgive and I would have been free. It was amazing.

Snapshot scenes of our lives can bind us, keeping us from what we long for. A few years of misery can turn into a lifetime of hell, if we let it. I was determined to find happiness, and be free.

Honestly, there is not one person in my life with whom I do not feel at peace when I think of them. Forgiveness doesn't mandate participation from both sides. If the other party doesn't want a ride on the forgiveness wagon I do it solo. It's about coming to a place of peace and allowing love to leak into my life again.

Harboring ill will made me sick. I was disconnected from my loving side. Operating from a place of love does not weigh me down, negative thinking does. Every time I do or say or think negative thoughts I am burdened. I carry that burden with me everywhere and into every relationship, until I shift my attitude.

Before the forgiveness step I did lick my wounds. Nurturing myself brought me to the place where I could see my own behavior. I needed to listen to my most vulnerable self, allowing her a voice despite her poor communication skills, and the rest became clear.

There are so many wonderful tools out there. If one tool didn't cut it I'd try something new. At first I felt selfish spending all this time on me, but I am worth it and so are all my relationships. Time spent on me means healthier relationships.

110

I learned the difference between Selfish with a capital S, and selfish with a small s. Capital S Selfish serves you; little s selfish doesn't.

For my efforts snippets of happiness started trickling into my life like sparkling diamonds dropping from the sky.

PARENTING

This child's life will affect many others,
and I must teach him as best I can.

Rebbe Menachem Mendel Schneerson – Toward
a Meaningful Life - Simon Jacobson

WHEN I was twelve years old my mother introduced me to *The Prophet* by Kahlil Gibran. It changed my life. We sat at the kitchen table reading each chapter aloud. The words on the page were alive. I felt as if I were talking to an old friend. It was familiar. Somewhere inside me hidden from view this friend was giving me the secrets of life.

One passage in his chapter on children spoke directly to my heart and nurtured my brokenness. 'Your children are not your children. They are the sons and daughters of Life's longing for itself. They come through you but not from you, and though they are with you, yet they belong not to you. You may give them your love but not your thoughts, for they have their own thoughts. You may house their bodies but not their souls, for their souls dwell in the house of tomorrow, which you cannot visit, not even in your dreams.'

At twelve I needed eternal Truth. I found it in those words. Regardless of what my life looked like I was free on the inside, no one could touch my soul. It was mine.

When I had children of my own I went back to the book. It taught me how to be a parent and what a sacred role that is. As parents, as Gibran describes, '*you are the bows from which*

113

your children as living arrows are sent forth'. Imagine being a bow used by God to sling the arrow, our child, into life.

My oldest son from my first marriage was seven years old when he came into my world, a tender little guy with no active mother in his world. I immediately felt I was born to be his bow and he was the arrow God gave me to send into the world. What a blessing.

What a sacred responsibility to shoot an arrow from God into the world. To be a mother giving home to three of God's souls and getting to love them as they wake up to their greatness and discover their purpose has been my greatest role.

Kahlil Gibran was a mentor sent to me when I needed it most. As Marsha Sinetar says in *The Mentoring Spirit*, 'we need not meet our mentors face-to face to learn from them or hear their news, their passions, their great 'I AM!' An unseen, timeless hook-up lets us receive each other's song. Truth wakes us up. It frees us. It stimulates our wholeness. No wonder we hunger for it.'

REASONS

The important thing is to not stop questioning.

Albert Einstein

GOD never does anything for one reason only. I'm always asking myself, what are the other reasons? What could this situation be opening me up to? Am I closing myself off to discovering another valley in the kingdom of 'Know Thy Self'?

When I can't figure out a reason I ask questions. Not that I'm privy to every reason, but when I ask, another reason usually reveals itself. My questions are simple, yet they produce answers if I'm willing to reflect, contemplate, and listen.

How am I serving this person or how is he or she serving me? Or, how can this be good? If it's bad, why is it bad? How could this happen? Why did it happen?

Acres and acres of experiences lay outside my front door. I don't have far to go to find something to chew on. I can pick any experience and find more than one meaning. What I thought had only one reason for happening may have more. What if there are more?

Contemplation and reflection... no wonder sages use those tools. I remember going to a retreat led by a sister from a priory in Olympia, Washington. A bowl was put in front of us with little pieces of paper folded over and on each one was written a Bible verse. After we picked a verse we were told to go walk the grounds reciting the verse out loud and in our mind. She gave us four hours to be alone with our verse. We were to spend time in silence to reflect and contemplate on how that verse applied to our lives.

When I first read the verse I wished I had picked another one. I didn't like it, but I kept it. I decided to give it a shot and see if this verse could reveal anything relevant to my life.

The exercise taught me a lot. It showed me how quickly I can get bored and anxious, and how quickly I think I know more than the exercise has to offer, and how much I want to quit before giving it a chance. It also showed me that when I take the time to look beyond my boredom and anxiousness there is a wise old sage waiting for me, willing to impart wisdom from my own inner kingdom.

After four hours of ruminating the verse, it came to life, applying to my relationships and helping me understand myself even more. I could share the verse here, but it isn't about the verse, it is about remembering when I spend time inside myself marrying my head and heart, contemplating, God speaks to me.

Why don't I do it more often? Why do I put anything else ahead of spending time with me? I don't know.

OBSERVING

I think we are frightened every moment
of our lives until we know Him

Hafiz – The Gift Poems by Hafiz,
Translations by Daniel Ladinsky

EVERY day or at least every other day I wonder if I'm heading in the right direction. There are moments I know I'm heading in the right direction, and moments I don't know a thing. How do two polar thoughts co-exist within me? Doubt and knowing, hand-in-hand acting as friends.

My heart is a horse whisperer. Watching me. She watches my wild stallion of behaviors and thoughts, observing until trust is built. When I feel safe enough, will I allow Her to guide my life?

Imagine what my life would look like if I used ten percent more of me, more of my potential, more of my love to serve the world. Imagine.

Am I more asleep than awake? Why is it easy for me to turn on the TV, to avoid me, to not listen, to numb myself to my heart? Why do I do that? What's in a gossip magazine that pulls me away?

I long to serve, yet a part of me shouts 'Don't'. Don't facilitate any more groups, cancel the class, cancel the workshop, just cancel everything and stay home. You're right, I reply. It would feel better, wouldn't it?

117

Thank goodness most of the time as the racket in my head rambles on I still get up, put my shoes on, and walk out the door. My heart knows better. I no longer let my feelings throw me back into the dreamy place between being alive and dead. I was dead too long. I'm not wasting any more of my life. I want to live life fully.

My mind likes to play worn out tapes. It loves old home movies. I've got to pay attention and not get caught up in the reels of film stored in my head. I've got to turn off the projector before I begin to forget what I know.

'Tell me what I know. Tell me what I know,' I plead to my friend when I'm in a cloudy mood.

All I need is one little sliver and I'll find my way out. I've always been good in the dark, making it from the bed to the toilet in the middle of the night with no stubbed toes, finding my way down the stairs when I hear a noise, or running to my kid's room without flipping on a light. I'm good at it.

Let me out.

Her voice somehow pierces the veil and I remember what I know. I'm out. I'm love. I'm back.

Re-entry doesn't blind my eyes-- it warms my face. I hear my soul singing deep inside of me and I join her song. Once again I am in harmony.

I am co-creating my life. I choose thoughts and actions that bring more love and laughter and joy to myself, and others. Remember, I tell myself, who you really are.

No longer will I be held captive. Far too long my sorrow and helplessness roamed throughout the 'The Kingdom of Overwhelmed' with a beggar's bowl. No more.

I feel the fresh air on my cheek and welcome Life's kiss. I am living heaven on earth.

118

I feel alive. Is this real? Will it last?

'Hurry,' I shout to Joe, to my family and friends, to my students, to those in my groups, 'hurry, join me in heaven.' Can you feel it? It's real. Hurry before I forget carried away by my thoughts and the lifeless reality of the past, hurry before I leave the land of awe where I love even my fat belly, hurry.

QUESTIONING GOD

The spiritual life does not come cheap. It is not a stroll down a Mary Poppins path with a candy-store God who gives sweets and miracles. It is a walk into the dark with the God who is the light that leads us through darkness.

Joan Chittister – Called to Question

MY husband Joe said, 'I don't believe there is a God. I believe things just happen. If God is supposed to be this loving person, why do innocent people get cancer and die, why are children molested and raped, why are innocents murdered? Why do these things happen? If there is a God, why doesn't this God give cancer to the child molesters and killers, the evil ones of society? I don't believe there is a God, things just happen.'

I lay in bed listening to him. I felt the same way. Joe has the ability to say what I often am afraid to even think. When I told him about my cousin being diagnosed with a rare and aggressive form of cancer Joe was filled with rage. Why does he have to go through this, why this insidious disease? He was saying it for both of us. It made no sense.

There I was, a person who talks to God every day, who tries to be the best I can be, questioning myself.

'Maybe you're right,' I answered slowly, allowing myself time to respond, rolling his words around in my head, my body, my heart, thinking the unthinkable. 'Maybe you're right. It makes no sense to me either. I can't prove that there is or isn't a God. All I know is I have to believe there is something. Believing things just happen and that all this is for nothing would plummet me into hopelessness. Then what good would I be to myself or you or the kids?'

We lay quietly thinking our own thoughts. We didn't speak. Eventually we fell asleep.

When I sat at my computer the next day I questioned my beliefs again. Who knows if any of what I'm writing is true, maybe I'm living in pure fantasyland. Who knows if there is an intelligent life force? Who knows why things happen? I don't.

Some cultures believe in multiple lives, in reincarnation. Maybe they're right, maybe they're wrong, who knows for sure? A lot of people are more fortunate than others, they have better health, more money and better living conditions. Why do some people have more? Is it because they deserve more? Why are we here in the United States? Why weren't we born in a third world country and made to struggle every day just to survive?

I don't know.

I know I have it better than a lot of people. I have time to spend contemplating, reflecting, pursuing my dreams and listening to my heart. My whole day is not an endless struggle to find food for myself, or my family.

I must complain less and do more. I must try not to get lost in worry, doubt, sadness, suffering; try to love more, be healthier and serve more. I must take advantage of the time I do have, if only to pray for others.

Use my time. Don't waste my time. Instead of wasting time, make it count for something, even if I choose to stay in bed all day with my husband, give hugs and lounge around on purpose, or get a book and make a hot cup of tea and soak in a story, let myself be taken away, enjoy it.

Enjoy my time whether it's doing nothing or doing something. Enjoy time more than complain about it.

I can't say whether I'd do better or worse in someone else's shoes. If, God forbid, I got diagnosed with a disease, or was crippled, or my child died, how would I react? Would I be able to fall back on any of the tools I use to anchor my life? I don't know.

I struggle with these questions as I write this. Is this book pointless? How will the questions and arguments I have with God serve others? My heart says write, so I write. Beyond that it's up to God. Is there a God?

ACTION

It is the plight of the mystic to enter the
universe of God alone where no charts or maps or
signs exist to guide us and assure us of the way.

Joan Chittister – Called to Question

I AM determined to become a deep thinker. It is a way to make sense out of why I was born. My goal is to reach inside of me, pull out all the raw material and make a life. A life filled with happiness.

The next step is to take action. Knowledge in itself won't bring me the happiness I long for. I have to bring everything I've learned into my day-to-day life.

Letting go of being a perpetual student, reading book after book and having a library every self-actualizing individual envied is tough. Stacking up knowledge means nothing if I don't have the courage to turn that knowledge into wisdom. The only way to create wisdom is to act on what you know. Action plus knowledge equals wisdom.

Rolling up my sleeves means living the Truth. Getting my hands dirty means being uncomfortable and responsible for my behavior. I'm strong enough to handle falling down again, and again. It's amazing, but when I fall down my knowledge emerges to help me work out the kinks of living my Truth.

There are periods when I get rid of all my books. That's it, 'I'm not reading another book', I'd say to myself. I box everything up and either give them away or turn them in to a second hand shop for a penny on the dollar. I don't care. When I'm full its time to get rid of the crutches.

It's so easy for me to escape into books. To study and ponder the discoveries of others, taking those discoveries and applying them to life takes some doing. Now when I catch myself escaping in an unhealthy way I recognize it in my body and in my emotions. I get a clogged feeling. I know when it's time to get out and live this stuff. I don't have to read about it again. Heck, I could write this stuff. I don't need another book.

Certain books stay on my shelves, but many of my page-filled friends have served their purpose and move on. Getting rid of books is like cleaning out the junk drawer.

Books will always be a part of my life. I love books. I feel good when they're around. I imagine their authors in the room with me. I envision them speaking all their glorious insights into my inner ear and wishing me great success as I live the happiness I believe I deserve.

When my husband goes out of town I love to bring a stack of books to bed and surround myself with them. I fall asleep imagining the authors talking to me all night long feeding me full of insights and discoveries in hopes that I, too, will own my greatness.

Eventually I'm back to buying books again, but I do take breaks.

When I live what I know I grow.

126

PROGRESS

I suspect there are destinations that call to us
from a secret place within ourselves and we
head for them instinctively.

Richard Bode – First You Have To Row A Little Boat

I know I'm making progress when I'm more aware of
heaven than hell. When I have more of those died-and-
gone-to-heaven moments than not, and when I see
God's face looking back at me in the faces of those I meet.
When I can look beyond the trappings of their hell and see
their unlimited potential or when I don't react but love
instead. I know I'm making progress.

127

AGELESS

REMEMBER albums, those round plastic discs that we had to play on a record player? Ever had a scratch on your favorite album, you know, where the needle gets stuck in a groove and repeats the same word or note over and over again? Annoying.

When something grates on me I become a not very nice person. That's what a rut can do, grate on your senses.

I hate not being my loving self. It feels uncomfortable. I'm a loving person. I'm happiest when I can be who I am. I'm miserable when I'm not.

Mainly, I work out of my home. During the week I get up early, go work out, come home and shower, put make-up on, and get dressed. Even though I work at home I get dressed up. Once in awhile I stay in my work-out duds, or my comfy clothes, but rarely.

Occasionally being in my comfy clothes is okay, but most days it's not. When I walk by a mirror and catch a glimpse of myself with straggly hair, no makeup, no shower, I go, 'yuck'.

I'm a better me when I make an effort to get dressed and look the best I can look. There is something about looking the best you can. It gives you an edge.

Once when I was teaching a class about job interviews I started sharing my routine of dressing up regardless of where I'm going. I said it made me feel better, that when I feel better I project better, I'm a better listener, a better speaker, or friend, whatever.

An older woman in class who was wearing sweats and no make-up, challenged me. 'Are you saying we have to wear make-up even when we don't feel like it? That if we don't wear make-up it can nix our chance for a job?'

I asked her, 'When you go to a special event, let's say a wedding, do you wear lipstick?

'Yes', she answered.

'Why?' I asked.

'Well, I feel better. I think I look prettier.'

As soon as she answered she started smiling. She got it.

It isn't about the make-up, it's about tying a ribbon around the whole package. When you feel you look prettier, you feel better. When you look your best you project your best.

We talked about staying in tune with the times. Not getting stuck in decades long gone. I loved the 80s and big hair. I was stuck in that decade far too long. If you can't look at yourself objectively, ask the opinion of someone you value.

I give myself makeovers every so often. When I changed my hair style from the big hair 80s and early 90s, to the straight, softer hair, it felt weird, but I felt more connected. I was in tune with the times and not lost in another era.

Some folks may say this is garbage. Who cares what you look like? My response would be, if it affects your esteem, your confidence, your ability to project from the core of your being, play with it, and see if changing something helps.

The woman who challenged me showed up at the following class wearing a light lip-gloss. The lip-gloss was so subtle I didn't notice it, but I noticed her. She had shifted, was more alive, more confident. She was smiling and talking more than usual to the other students. She pulled me aside after class and said, 'You know, wearing lip-gloss does make me feel more professional.'

My reply was, 'You are a professional, you finally own it and it shows.'

Whatever it takes for us to claim the positive aspects of ourselves I say let's go for it. Adding a touch of the latest and greatest gives me youthful energy. I may be in my 50s but I feel like I'm in my 30s. I'm ageless.

Ageless. What a great space to be in. Kind of like mysterious. You give off a mystique, a confidence about yourself. It makes you a magnet. Others gravitate towards you.

Okay, sign me up.

It's so much easier to stay in my work-out clothes than to go upstairs and get dressed, but is the cost worth it? Some days it is. Weekends are times when I will go either way.

I've been married for several years but I still want to be the gorgeous princess my husband fell for. I want to leave a bit of intriguing essence floating in the ether. When I look my best I feel sexy. It doesn't matter if 'my' sexy doesn't match Victoria's Secret sexy; my sexy is my sexy, it's good.

Appealing is great. When I feel myself to be appealing I am more connected to my heart. Some days it doesn't matter, but most days it does.

These are things I've learned over the years. In addition to my spiritual treasures I tie in the physical, mental, and emotional treasures, too. They are all one.

131

When I exercise I feel better about me. I know it's not all about feelings, we are much more than feelings, but if good feelings help you get what you seek why not?

I seek happiness so I'm using it all.

DISCERNMENT

Learning how to thrive requires much
thought and reflection.

Larry Wilson & Hersch Wilson – Play to Win

DOES love mean being a mushball? No. It means being the best I can for myself and for whomever Life puts in my path. It is being accountable for my actions. It isn't always easy being the best for others. Sometimes it means they won't like what they hear or see.

Doing the right thing requires discernment. Listening. Being quiet. Trusting myself despite the emotions flailing about to and fro.

On those windy days when fear flaps in my face and worry runs along side jumping up and down, anxiousness nips at my heels. On days like that I pray to be made aware of my emotions. It's easy to run around on auto pilot reacting. It takes courage to stop, listen, and change course.

All I can do is break my own mold and be the best of what I've got.

UNKNOWN

Once suffering is acknowledged, it can be dealt with.
If left repressed or denied, however, suffering only festers
and pushes the pain deeper than ever.

Gary Howard - We Can't Teach What We Don't Know

W HEN new ideas show up my mind shows me how crazy the idea is. It reminds me in detail how often I've tried similar feats and failed. But no more, things are a changing.

Every experience is card catalogued. The placement of the card depends on how much time I've spent thinking about it, not necessarily when the experience occurred.

When I think up a new adventure, cards of like experiences remind me of previous outcomes. If they were negative I'm reminded how we failed, were laughed at or were rejected.   Most of the cards at the front of the catalog are of negative experiences. The positive experiences fell towards the back, because I seem to dwell on the negatives.

Learning how the mind worked was a top priority. One thing I have in my favor as an adult that I didn't have as a kid is awareness.

Finding happiness meant changing myself completely. I had to leave my habitual way of thinking and build a new foundation. I had to enter Uncomfortable Land.

When I jump back into the driver's seat with the intention to love myself, fear has to move to the back seat.

Fear loves to nag, but I am in charge, I have my foot on the accelerator and my hands on the wheel.

My heart showed me I could reorganize the card catalog. The first step was to watch my thoughts. What a boring job, and so time consuming. I soon found out how impatient I am.

When a thought pops up I try to catch it and ask myself, does this thought serve me? What will it take to turn that negative thought into a positive? Is it a matter of discipline and stopping myself or is there something about the remark that needs to be addressed?

I find replacements for the negative thoughts. If my mind keeps going over a negative experience, I ask myself, is there another reason why it happened? Usually I say no only to discover later I was wrong. But asking the question creates an opening for other reasons to show up and shift my opinion.

Life will bring someone into my life with my same story but a different outcome. Or I'll read a like story in a book or see it acted out in a movie and there's another twist to the outcome, making me aware there are more reasons. With several different reasons presented it makes me rethink my position.

Now when I ask myself why the experience happened I am much slower with my 'know-it-all' answers.

Awareness, awareness, awareness is the key. By being open and becoming more aware of what I think, changes happened, some obvious, some not.

The majority of my changes like all changes when you are waiting for them to happen seem like they take forever, but as I look back the shifts occurred quickly when I accepted the need for change. My 'aha' moments I use as markers for moving closer to my goal. The more frequent the 'ahas,' the closer I am and the more happiness I experience.

Being positive takes work. In a negative-driven society being positive takes a good deal of energy. There are great days followed by days in the thick of negativity.

Judging myself based on the events of one day is wrong. Averages work best. Did I have more happy days this month compared to last month, more 'aha' moments than the month before?

I don't know why it's human nature to think of all the bad things versus the good, but it's true. Didn't matter how many compliments I received, if someone said something negative, even slightly, that was the experience I dwelled on.

'Oh, Sandy you look great today', said by several people would be cancelled out by one person asking, 'Are you feeling okay? You don't look well'. I'd think about that comment for hours. The 'Oh Sandy you look great today' comments would slip into the back of the card catalog never to be seen again.

Breaking habits is uncomfortable. It's not easy to change. It takes courage and commitment and I'm proud of myself for doing whatever it took to turn my life around. It felt unnatural at first to talk about positive things when overall life didn't feel so positive.

I am grateful that loving is what I was born to do. I know being negative does not serve my goal of being happy. My next step was to acknowledge my negative emotions.

I thought negative emotions were my enemy. It took me years to realize they were my friends. They were the ones who kept trying to get my attention when I wanted to ignore a past wound or one I thought was already healed.

I quit beating myself up because I was negative. I tried different things. Treating my anger, sadness or frustration like it was a person and asking why are you here, what do you want to share with me helped. When I acknowledge the presence of my emotion I put it on the table where I can deal with it. Acknowledging takes the power out of the emotion, it realizes you are listening and doesn't have to work so hard. If I denied the emotion and pushed it out of sight it would come out eventually in a more determined way.

Old habits wait in the wings looking for a stage. Unresolved wounds don't wait, they find a way out. Listening to my body and scanning my emotions is part of my daily life.

One of my prayers is, 'make me aware of any unresolved wounds. Please, help me recognize the presence of my emotions so I may give them the attention they deserve and transform them into peaceful memories.'

Being aware that old habits do come back, and not getting cocky over my triumphs is another learning curve. I give thanks for each triumph. If not for the still small voice inside me I would not be living heaven on earth. I proclaim my deepest gratitude each day.

It is easy to fall back to the old ways if you're not paying attention.

Outside influences are powerful. Every day I'm exposed to someone claiming to have the formula for a happy life. When I'm feeling weak sometimes I believe it.

It's pounded into my head day after day. I need to be driving a car like this, have so much money in the bank, have a body that looks young and youthful, and live in a grand house with perfect children and a perfect partner. Advertisers, moviemakers, magazine publishers, and the music industry all survive by feeding on our emotions. Snake oil salesmen declare that images I see or the words that I read are true.

They are wrong. No one outside of me has the perfect formula for happiness. My formula is inside me, waiting for me to claim it.

Snake oil salesman beware, I've got your number. Now if I choose to use your products it will be because I want to not because I need to. I am on guard with heightened awareness so I don't fall prey to your mesmerizing ways.

Happiness is not about what I have or don't have. It's not about what life has done for me or how lucky or unlucky I am. It's not about anything outside me. It's about embracing the love in my heart and using that love to help me experience happiness despite the chaos.

The day I found happiness I was living in a twenty-year old house carpeted with orange shag, I was driving a second-hand car and had nothing in the bank. Those things did not determine the happiness in my life. I opened the door to happiness inside my heart and my world has never been the same.

When an experience has a grip on me, instead of fighting it I ask myself questions. Why am I thinking about it? Is there a part of me that needs healing? Putting it on the table allows me to look into the experience and see what is waiting to be revealed.

If I need healing then I do whatever it takes. Depending on the pain associated with the experience it may take moments or it may take much longer to begin the healing process. Regardless of what life throws my way I know a force more powerful dwells in me. It is love.

Healing a painful experience does not mean forgetting. It means entering a sacred space where that experience finds its way home eventually to become a peaceful memory. Misery has no permanent place in my life. I am determined to find happiness.

For the rest of my life I will use the strength of love to transform life's fireballs. Pain, whether experienced thirty years ago or yesterday, if left unresolved stays in the front of the card catalog and expresses itself through new experiences until it gets my attention. I am now sensitive to this process and am much quicker to respond.

One tool I've used to shift from negative to positive focus is engaging my silliness. When I get in the car I pull down the visor, look in the mirror, and tell myself how dang cute I am. I follow it up by saying I love you while looking myself straight in the eye.

The first time I did it I cried. I'd never said I love you while looking at my reflection. A friend once told me if you stare at yourself in the mirror long enough you eventually see your soul. I did. There She was behind my eyes and She stared back at me. She was so gentle and She loved me. I could feel it.

Before long I was doing it all the time and, even though at first I didn't believe it, eventually I did. I started feeling the words. I believed them. I did love me.

It became a fun habit. I'd end up laughing out loud at how silly I was. To this day my attitude perks up every time I do it. Now my grandkids are part of the game. When they get in my car they watch Nana pull down the visor and talk sexy to herself, 'oh Nana, you look so good I could kiss you.' Then I kiss myself on the visor mirror. Soon the car is filled with laughter and Nana gets a chance to talk about loving ourselves, and how that gives us energy to do what we need to do every day.

Making a habit of noticing the good things, the positives, is finally natural for me. I made it a habit. I soak in the compliment I'm given and I acknowledge myself for a job well done. I share positive experiences with friends. By talking about it and thinking about it, and getting the story out of my body I anchor the experience to the front of my card catalog as an important memory. A positive experience I easily access when I venture out with a new idea. 'See we did it before, we can do it again.'

I'm proud of myself. I risked and my life is better for it. I'm training my mind that stepping into the unknown is a good thing. I have the tools and the know-how to make whatever happens work out for the best. I can do it. That's not ego; that is who I am.

I've had a lot of catching up to do. My past was dominated with the negative behavior, but acknowledging that behavior has paid off. My mind goes along with me responding positively or negatively depending on the energy I give it. It doesn't care, but I do.

I live a more positive life and I'm reaping its fruit. At my age I'm over my youthful years. I'm into my sage years with not a moment to spare. If I want it, I better go after it or shut my mouth. There are no excuses. I make my heaven or my hell on earth. No one else will do it for me. I must carve out my niche, my sense of well-being, and create my happiness. All it takes is hard work.

My card catalog is filled with risk adventures, stepping out into the unknown and thriving. It's about handling rejection and being better for it. It's about experiencing pain and using that pain to serve my life instead of take from it. I have many cards of courage, love and strength, and they are all in the front of my catalog. When I want to jump off the pier and try something new I'm shown how we did it in the past and succeeded. I go for it with more enthusiasm than anxiety.

In the back of my catalog my resolved broken pieces are at home where they live as peaceful memories ready to help others when needed. I call them spirit stories, stories of healing from the heart. I use them, sharing how they became steppingstones for the next leg of my growth. By sharing them they continue to be anchored in my past as peaceful memories where they can stay for the rest of my life.

TIME

All I have seen teaches me to trust the
Creator for all I have not seen.

Ralph Waldo Emerson

WHEN we came home from a three-week
vacation in Mexico I immediately felt guilty for
living in such a big house. In Mexico our maid
invited us to visit her family in the mountains where her
mother, father, sisters, and cousins lived and where she had
grown up. She worked as a maid in the coastal resort town
to earn money for her children.

Maria (the name I will give her for this story), and I hit it
off the first day we met. I had two huge suitcases filled with
clothes I brought and wanted to give to the local church. I
pointed to the bags and with the help of my Spanish
dictionary I asked Maria where the local church was. I was
trying to tell her that I wanted to give these clothes to the
poor not realizing at the time she was poor.

The suitcases were filled with stylish designer dresses
made from beautiful fabrics. Before leaving on our trip I had
asked members of a group I was facilitating if they would
pick out a favorite article of clothing and let me take it to
Mexico to donate to the poor. I was reminded how easy it is
to give away something you don't use or are tired of, but to
let go of something you still want, that is where we truly
grow.

143

Maria's eyes showed her disbelief. She kept asking me if I was sure I wanted to give these clothes away. Yes, I said, to the church, but if she would like to have two outfits from the suitcase it would please me. We had so much fun as she tried on outfit after outfit, and finally chose the ones she wanted.

The next day came the invitation to visit her family in the mountains and we set a date. Maria's French Canadian brother-in-law told us the ride was through drug lord territory, but not to worry, nothing would happen. 'How do you know that', I asked? He laughed and replied, 'If you think it will, it will, if you think it won't it won't.'

For that reason I worked on positive thinking all the way up the mountain.

We crossed over two dry riverbeds and made our way up a dirt trail to their home. When we arrived Mamma came running toward us waving hands covered with orange soil from her repair of one of the adobe walls. When we approached the porch, the grandfather, who was on a hammock, immediately got off and offered it to us.

We didn't speak Spanish and they didn't speak English, but with help from our French Canadian friend and a lot of hand signals and facial expressions we spent a 'never will forget' afternoon. We were welcomed and loved. We laughed and laughed, all of us having the best of times. National Geographic had nothing on us.

Maria's sister, the one married to the French Canadian, fell in love with her man one summer when he ventured into their town on his off-season. He was a truck driver for a Canadian company. When he saw her that was it, they married and have been together ever since. He owned the dented old lime green spray painted Volkswagen Beetle that we used to make the trip. It was the only car in the family of twelve adult siblings and all their children. He was a hero to them all.

Our trip to visit Maria's parents was multi-purposed. The rainy season was approaching and no one would be able to get down the mountain except by donkey. Straddled between four adults in the cramped vehicle were 100lb bags of sugar and flour, and plenty of candy for the kids and Grandpapa.

Mamma brought out chairs and a cool drink she had made from limes and water, water they carried from their well in ten-gallon jugs balanced on their heads.

As we sat there sipping our drinks the women were busy shucking corn for tortillas. I offered to help. At first they motioned me to rest but I kept grinning and gesturing that I would love to help them prepare supper. Mamma smiled and eventually pulled a wooden crate next to her and motioned for me to sit there. Around our feet many ears of corn lay in a box next to a large pile of cornhusks. Her big smile encouraged me to keep trying and I not only learned how to shuck the dry corn, but how to grind it, and make tortillas in a kitchen with a hole in the roof for smoke.

Chickens ran in and out of the house along with the children from families living on this beautiful mountain. We were told that if we spent the time to dig in the land we'd find ruins from civilizations of long ago. They said ghosts lived on the land and if you listened you could see and hear the spirits. I tried but I couldn't hear anything.

All the children laughed at me as I sat at the stone table attempting to make one simple tortilla shell. Finally after my fourth try a single shell appeared and everyone clapped, even Grandmamma was giggling.

145

They were the most gracious people. We were honored to spend time with them in their home and surroundings experiencing their lives. I knew in my heart we were being blessed with more than a typical Mexican vacation. In time more would be revealed. And it was.

As I already mentioned, the first revelation was when we got home we felt we had too many things. We live in a big house-- just the two of us with all our stuff. I went to work simplifying, cleaning out closets and learning to live with less. I was determined to be more aware of what we have and to value each possession we purchase.

The second revelation that hit me was about the gift we were given at birth to be born and raised in a country with so much opportunity. This revelation was the strongest. I mulled it over for months. The people we met were living like we did a hundred years ago. They used their time for the basic necessities. I, on the other hand, had extra time and the question kept creeping into my heart, what was I doing with my time?

Was this about gratitude only? I was sure it wasn't. Yes, I was grateful for what I had, but there was more. What was I doing with the luxury of time?

An inner urgency beckoned my action. Born in a country of riches, evolved to a point of having extra time, the question haunted me. How was I spending my time? Was I crying over spilt milk or was I doing whatever it took to use this gift to serve others?

The story of Adam and Eve kept coming back to me. They had it all, Eden, paradise, but they didn't know it was paradise. They didn't realize they could create anything they wanted to. They didn't get it. They didn't know they could be creators. They had to have everything taken away before they discovered their abilities.

What if God kicked them out so they could discover their authentic selves and add to paradise, taking paradise to a whole new level? What if?

It made sense to me.

Adam and Eve kicked out of paradise into a land filled with unknowns where they had to rely on their own abilities. They had to make clothes and find shelter. They did what they had to do and now we're here.

Some people make use of their time adding to the world; others die bitter and cold, worrying about everything and never getting anywhere.

I didn't want to be one of the latter.

I was not going to waste any more time. Spending my time aware would serve me, and those around me, regardless of what I was doing.

The more I contemplated this gift the more gratitude I had for our trip and the wonderful people we met. I thought about my own ancestors, my great, great grandmother and grandfather, my mother and father, and the opportunities each generation has to take life to the next level and serve in incredible ways. I felt my ancestors standing on the other side of the invisible veil between here and there sending me their love, saying yes, Sandy, we are passing the baton to you, use your time wisely, make the most of it. We love you.

Time. Do not waste this gift. Use time to serve the world in your unique way.

I KNOW THAT

No man can reveal to you aught but that which
already lies half asleep in the dawning of your knowledge.

Kahlil Gibran – The Prophet

I can't hear myself think when I'm on information overload. It's as though I have a zillion parts of me screaming for attention, wanting to talk, but no one is listening. When I stop to listen I feel the release. It becomes quiet on the homefront and I'm able to reconnect with my heart.

When teaching my students about professional development I tell them, 'you've paid big bucks for this class but what I'm going to teach you, you already know. I will share with you some tricks on how to access what you know.'

When I hear others imparting words of wisdom, I listen and part of me gobbles it down as if it were popcorn at the movies. When I'm done I sit back and tell myself, 'I knew that.' And the truth is, I did.

Truth rings like a gong clanging inside me. The understanding I get gives words to what I already know. Those are 'aha' moments, confusion turning into understanding.

What if we have a beacon inside us constantly sending out light signaling to the world exactly what we need? Maybe a book or a person or an experience we are relating to is not

149

because we're lucky, but because our beacon of light directed it to us.

The saying 'when you're ready the teacher will appear' is true. Why don't we pat ourselves on the back more often when we finally muster the courage and strength to heal our suffering?

It's easier to do nothing than something. It takes courage to get raw and real. Running on overload doesn't serve anybody. Getting to our knowing gives us clarity and with clarity we have more energy to act on what we know.

Isn't it time to get to your place of knowing? Your happiness depends on it.

HEALING

I found out, almost after it was too late, that my children
weren't born to learn from my experiences;
they were born to learn from their own, and any attempts on my
part to substitute my perceptions for
theirs was doomed to fail.

Richard Bode – First You Have to Row a Little Boat

ONCE when talking to my daughter who at the
time was in her twenties, I could hear her
resistance to what I was saying. I remember
having that same resistance toward my mother when I was
my daughter's age.

We were talking about healing. We were talking about
our dads and our wounds of the past. She said she'd healed
the wounds between her and her father. I told her how
happy I was for her and that at her age I'd thought the same
thing. I went on to say that the older I got the more work I
realized needed to be done. She assured me there was no
deeper place to go. She said I was making her feel as though
she still held a grudge towards her dad. That was not my
intention, I said; my intention was to share my journey of
how healing continues and unfolds the older you get.

We changed the subject. Healing is a solo gig. The time to
offer my two cents is when I'm asked, not before.

Many times I want to share with my kids how I made it
through a similar experience, but they don't want to hear it.

My kids must go elsewhere to find their way. It is part of
growing up. It's healthy to develop a sense of confidence, of
self-assurance, and to work through your wounds in your
own time. My journey is a road map. If they want to use it
they will; if they don't, that's okay too.

Easy to say, but my neediness still gets in the way at times.
I want to share so my kids will have an easier time. But it's
their journey. They've lived different circumstances. Our
walks are different. I had my mother and father, my
childhood; they experienced their own. The only way for
them to find real value is to figure it out on their own, and
live what they discover.

When I doubt or worry I remember they had me for a
mother, a person who tried with all her ability to put them
first, to love them. I'm part of their foundation, warts and all.

Sharing our healing journey often begins outside our inner
family circle. We make new families in order to nurture our
tender spots. We create relationships or experiences to
express our pain. Often others can use that information, in
fact even are eager for it.

I take comfort in Jesus' story. He had to go outside his
hometown to preach, to share his Truths with others. In his
own town he was plain old Jesus. You know, Mary's kid, the
guy who liked to hammer nails. I can hear them in my
mind, 'Oh Jesus, he's always been that way, that goofball.
Listen to him as he goes on and on.'

Imagine.

My need to share with my kids and protect them is
absurd. Who am I protecting them from, the bogey man?
They must walk their own experiences. They are as capable
of eternal Truth as I am. I can't do it for them. I can only
love them as they walk their own lives.

If they come to me and ask, that's great, but if they don't then I need to make that okay, too.

When my oldest was in his thirties he started calling me and asking questions. I was thrilled. Wow, what a concept, ask old Mom what she thinks. It was refreshing to be able to share with a child eager to hear and ready to listen.

My mother is dead, but my father is alive. He's in his seventies and I'm in my fifties. I am eager for his wisdom and discoveries he's made along his path. He doesn't talk in those terms, but when he shares a story I listen and take away precious gems for my pouch. I value and cherish him and have learned to be creative in my listening techniques.

Back in my youth, I didn't want to talk to him or hear his wisdom. I wanted something else from him. I needed to lick my wounds and heal myself. That took time. But when I did, I found the ears and eyes of my heart and with it the bonus of understanding. I was able to experience his love. A love that never stopped, despite my doubts, a love that has been mine since birth.

I am grateful I had the courage to heal. Two blessings received for my efforts, a profound love and appreciation for my mother and my father. Before my mother died I was able to love her and be loved by her with amazing closeness. And now I have a great relationship with my dad. It is close in ways deeper than I ever imagined. I am forever grateful.

We value each other.

My children are unique as we all are. They process things differently than I do. They perceive life through different lenses. They know I am there for them watching their backs. If they ever do need me I know that's a comfort. It is always a comfort knowing someone's watching your back, at least it is for me.

EVERYTHING SERVES

The unexamined life is not worth living.

Socrates

THIS morning I felt ready to hibernate. I ate a bag of microwave popcorn and climbed back into bed. I called a friend. Tell me what I know, please tell me what I know. I burst into tears.

There are days when regardless of your practice you feel weak, failure bells start ringing, you're not sure you are going in the right direction. On those days we need a support team. Mine consists of three dear friends, my husband, and select members of my family.

I don't need help from those incapable of giving me what I need. When I'm trying something new I turn to those whom I know will cheer me on, not hammer my idea into the ground. I turn to the same cheerleaders when I need reconnection. I need to have someone tell me he or she loves me, that I'm strong, that I'm connected to God, that I'm in exactly the right spot; or I need them to say nothing and listen to me.

In addition to my support team I have what I call my heart basket. It's filled with notes from clients, family, and friends telling me how much I mean to them. There are many days when the words on those cards battle my thoughts on how rotten I am. They feed me and help get me out of my negative self talk and back into the driver's seat.

My spiritual walk, which is my heart work, always includes ways to bring me back into Life's arms. I read about other spiritual seekers and how they struggle and it makes me feel good to know they have down days too. A Catholic priest, Henri Nouwen, who wrote several thought provoking books suffered many days of being down, wondering if he was serving. If he only knew how many days he has touched my life. His being real was a comfort to me. Even down days serve the greater whole in positive ways. They show us we're human and we experience human emotions. Nobody is 'up' all the time so quit beating yourself up because you're having a down day.

In one of Henri Nouwen's books, *The Inner Voice of Love*, he says, 'Your willingness to experience your powerlessness already includes the beginning of surrender to God's action in you. When you cannot sense anything of God's healing presence, the acknowledgement of your powerlessness is too frightening. It is like jumping from a high wire without a net to catch you.'

There are many days when I don't feel God's healing presence.

I remember a woman saying to me, 'it sure feels good to hear you say you're having a bad day'. I was surprised. She said, 'sometimes you seem so up, so connected, always one with your heart, and it makes me feel inadequate'.

Even though we can't make anyone feel one way or the other, I knew what she meant.

It got me thinking. What if down moods serve, too?

Her words taught me that other people feel bad when they can't pull themselves out of a funk, too. It wasn't just me thinking I wasn't doing enough. We need to hear about struggling as well as happiness. We experience both.

I fall into pits as often as anyone else. I may not stay down as long, but that's only because I work on listening to my heart and being aware of myself all the time.

Life is filled with cycles, being down is one of them. Some people fall harder than others. When I fall I'm glad I have my spiritual life to cushion me.

Ever since I was a kid I've been seeking, asking questions, trying to make sense of the adult world. Wondering why people acted the way they did. But it took my mom's death and me hitting the pavement to make me adamant about assembling a magic carpetbag of tools to use when life throws another fireball my way.

There are many people who don't like to deep-sea dive into reflection and contemplation. They run from exploring the depths of the spiritual sea and focus on other things. All I know is it's my walk. It's what I do.

If I can lend others a shoulder in life, or a mirror for them to see their greatness I am tickled. I'm doing my work. I heard the other day it's not what we do, but the spirit we bring to what we do that others will remember.

I sometimes wonder if I got in a wreck and was paralyzed or was diagnosed with a terminal disease and was bed-bound, what would I do? I wonder after dancing with my demons, if I ever could escape them, if I could figure out a way to be in service? I wonder if I was bored to tears or felt completely useless if I would be able to find my way or would I even care? I hope I would.

Maybe I could still pray for others, or be in a place of acceptance allowing others to help me, bathe me, feed me. I don't know if I could do it, but I hope I'd try. To live the best I could with whatever I had, wouldn't that be a miracle?

157

I've experienced others who do it. Their light shines. Even though they appear helpless, they're not. They keep me vigilant on my path.

Who knows what I would or wouldn't do? Those thoughts roll around in my brain. They serve me. They keep me in a place of gratitude for what I have and keep me on my path. You never know what life will unleash.

LISTENING TO LIFE

Outside lies utterly ordinary space
open to any casual explorer willing to find the extraordinary.

John Stilgoe - Outside Lies Magic: Regaining History
and Awareness in Everyday Places.

JOHN Stilgoe, a professor at Harvard was on 60 Minutes a few years ago. I was fascinated by the interview. He seems to be a man who uses the power of observation. He believes ordinary objects and places are anything but ordinary if you use your eyes and look closely to really observe them.

He teaches his students to look around to discover more than what first meets the eye. He stopped distributing schedules of his lectures which frustrated his students. His focus was to encourage students to explore, to be present to what arises in the moment and follow that lead. Alumni claim he taught a technique they continue to use throughout their lives. It is a way of seeing life.

Observation is a key. If life were a treasure chest, an observation key would lie inside. Observing yourself and your surroundings provides clues to mysteries that have you stumped. If we can go outside and discover magic, think about what we'd find if we explored the landscape within.

The past serves us. It can harm or help; everything is a double-edged sword. Our strengths can get out of balance if we don't pay attention. If we have the gift of gab, it can serve or harm others. If we have the gift of giving, we can get so

159

drained that we become resentful. If our intuition is fairly good, we can get cocky and quit listening.

The chief of the Cowlitz tribe is Roy Wilson. He is also the spiritual shaman of that tribe, and was a Methodist pastor for forty years. He told me something I will never forget.

One time my husband Joe was working in Alaska. We had been studying with Roy and learning about the medicine wheel and other teachings. While he was driving to work with his boss, Joe's boss pointed out the window and shouted, 'Joe, look, a feather.'

Sure enough floating in the air in front of their truck was an eagle feather. His boss who was driving put on the brakes, jumped out of the truck, and grabbed the feather before it touched the ground. When he got back into the truck he gave it to Joe. He said, 'Here. You keep it, you're more into this than I am.'

When Joe got home from Alaska he didn't tell me about the experience until the day of our anniversary. He sat me down and handed me a red cloth folded in thirds. I opened the cloth and inside was the eagle feather. It was then I heard the story. He told me he knew the feather was meant for me, not him.

This eagle feather had never touched the ground. Symbolizing the Great Mystery, Father Sky, God, the eagle is a sacred bird. As I held the eagle feather I hugged Joe. What a gift.

The following day I called Roy Wilson, the spiritual leader of his tribe, to ask him what it meant for me to receive such a gift.

He said, 'Sandy, you have been given eagle powers. You will know and see things you have never known before, these powers are a gift from the eagle.'

I was silent. His voice then got deeper and louder. 'One thing you must remember. These powers are a gift to you. They came from the eagle. If you claim the powers as your own they will leave you as quickly as they came. Remember this always.'

I have never forgotten his words. I believe any insight I'm given comes from God. It is meant to serve. If I ever abuse that gift I will lose it.

As Roy Wilson says in his book *Medicine Wheels*, 'as we realize that the Great Spirit dwells in all of us we must accept the responsibility to ourselves and to our fellow humans to allow these powers to flow through us to others.'

Responsibility comes with deepening your intuition. We must act on it. We can't be afraid to use the gift. If we are afraid, God will use someone else to deliver the message.

Awareness starts out small but gains momentum. It's as if life is testing us. Will you really use the information I'm giving you or not? If not, no big deal; I'll find someone who will.

As a wee one my intuition was pretty well oiled, but life eventually knocked the wind out of me. I didn't trust my insights. They were too tainted having looked through unresolved negative experiences inside me. When my mother died and my foundation crumbled I vowed to discover my authentic self and rebuild my life.

The more I healed the more I began to trust myself. Putting on lenses of optimism gave me healthier perspectives. One day when I still had my shop a customer came in. I got a gut level feeling that I was supposed to tell her something. I kept hearing in a way without words that 'the children appreciate her work'.

Was this the message I was supposed to give her?

I knew it was but kept arguing with myself. I can't tell her that; I don't even know this woman, she'll think I'm nuts.

'No problem', I heard my heart say, 'we'll find someone else to give her the message'.

No, no, I want to do it.

As she walked around the store my stomach churned. Okay, when should I approach her, what was I going to say? I kept writing the message on a piece of paper 'the children appreciate your work'.

When she approached the counter I blurted out, 'You may think this is strange, but I must tell you the children appreciate your work.'

'Of course they do,' she replied. Then she paused staring at me. 'How do you know?'

I told her I wasn't sure.

She broke into tears. She told me she was a therapist to severely brain-damaged children. A few months prior she'd come to Seattle to interview for a job to work with these kids and decided to take it despite some reservations. She'd only been here a few months but felt she was making progress with these kids who couldn't communicate.

I was stunned. We both cried. I had no idea how I knew, I just knew. It was as if these kids who couldn't talk found a way to communicate, an unconventional way, but nevertheless a way. I listened and acted. She received the gift. We were both validated. She was validated for following her heart to relocate here and to work with these children and I knew it was right to act on what my heart was whispering.

It wasn't because I was special that I was given the message. If I had not spoken up, I'm sure she would have received the message somehow. But because I had the

162

courage to speak I got to participate in this incredible exchange, an intimate acknowledgment of pure love.

The more connected we become with our inner landscape, the more we will bring that connection into everything we think, say, and do.

Have you gone swimming in your inner lakes? Have you experienced the valleys, the cliffs and meadows of your inside passage? What territory is there yet to discover inside you? Do you have the desire to become a spiritual pioneer and serve not only yourself but others in ways you have never imagined?

MAKING SPACE

How we spend our days is, of course,
how we spend our lives.

Annie Dillard

C LEARING out my closets, cleaning my house, giving away things I treasure serves me. By clearing out the old I make way for the new. I clear out my thoughts and I clear out my house. When I can't clear my head I clean a room. Before I know it, by organizing a place in my home I've organized and cleared space in my head too.

I have a dear friend who says that when you rearrange your furniture or add something to a room you need to create a scene. The scene should tell its own story and set the stage for an experience.

All over my house are little scenes. Groupings of pictures, a special lamp and a book, even how I've placed the toaster with the fruit bowl next to it. Anywhere you walk in my house you'll find a scene, something to draw you in, anywhere but my closet.

My closet is a work in progress, things come in and things go out. I'm a try-on-three-outfits-before-I'm-satisfied type of gal. There are days when all goes well, but most days I try on one outfit, look at myself, and try on something else.

Every two months or so I get an urge to clean out my closet and get rid of things. If I haven't worn it for a year, it's gone.

The process is symbolic. I release something physical (the article of clothing), and it seems something emotional is released at the same time.

Why does an old coat I haven't worn in years still have power over me? Sure I paid a lot of money for it, but it doesn't fit and it's out of style. Is it because I watch my pennies? Is it because I think I'll fit into it someday? I finally realized that if I'm not using it, it's stagnant energy. Someone else could be using it. Let it go, breathe life back into it; let it go.

Even cleaning out a junk drawer makes me feel better. I've brought order to some area of my life that usually shifts my attitude about everything. I've created space.

Everything in our house reflects our heart. Less is more. Clutter attracts clutter. Space attracts space. I need room to give birth to my ideas, to create the life of my choosing, to feel the wholeness of my being.

Clearing out is part of my spiritual practice. I make room for the new.

Should I be clearing out people too?

HAPPINESS

I believe that the very purpose of our
life is to seek happiness.

His Holiness the Dalai Lama – Art of Happiness

HAPPINESS is contagious. It seems when I'm happy those around me are happier. My happiness creates an environment where others, if they want, can choose to live from their greatness. Being happy brings out my calm demeanor. I am more accepting and encouraging. I acknowledge positive qualities in others. My love shines brighter when I'm happy and it reaches into dark corners.

Happiness breeds itself.

How is that possible? People don't have to put up defenses or build walls around their vulnerability when they are met with happiness. They don't have to combat reactions emotional wounds can trigger.

When I smile my face lights up. People pick up on non-verbal behavior and usually respond from the same place within their being.

What if the Dalai Lama is right, we are to seek happiness?

Is it wrong to be happy when we see so much sadness around us? If we are sad how does that serve those around us?

Getting mired in the madness around us is a societal norm. Violence, speed, aggression, instant gratification

167

attitudes abound. How can we not help but step into the flow of what's presented to us day after day? Everyone else is. Buttons get pushed and emotions ignite.

I was talking with a friend about healthcare and her thoughts provoked my questions. She believes the body has an amazing ability to heal itself in most circumstances. When we get a fever, it's for a reason. When we have a headache, the body is telling us something.

When did we stop listening?

Why do we run for the quick fix, discounting the body's amazing intelligence? What if the body is talking to us, sharing with us the secrets for a healthy life? What if symptoms presented are clues about our lifestyle? What if they are talking to us about what we put into our mouths and minds? What if those symptoms are asking us to pay attention to our eating, to slow down, to get some exercise? Why are we quick to alleviate the symptom only to have it manifest in some other way, some other time?

Happiness is not a smiley face. Healing our bodies takes time and discomfort, so does happiness. It requires us not to seek instant gratification, but to listen to our bodies, our minds, and our spirit. Happiness emerges from the harmony created when we do.

My husband was reading the newspaper out loud one day. He was getting upset over the killings taking place all over the world. His voice was loud, his anger clear. I asked him not to read the story to me. Upset with the atrocities mankind inflicts on one another, he snapped back, 'Don't you care about what's happening?'

I stood at the kitchen sink washing the dishes thinking about his words.

168

'Yes I care.' I responded. 'That's why I don't want to hear about it over and over again, or read about it every day. I'm aware of the killing and horrors of the world. How can I not be? The media is filling our heads with it minute-by-minute, blow by blow. How does it serve those being killed if I become filled with rage? My being angry is not going to change the world; it will only add to the chaos around me. I am trying as hard as I can to be a safe harbor in the midst of the storm. When I am at peace I radiate peace. I think more clearly, I am kinder to those around me. I model what I believe the world needs.'

He listened as I went on.

'Your rage will serve if you do something with it. Join a peace march or write your political representatives, even the President, or start a fundraiser to help victims. That is a good use of your rage. But if your rage only upsets you, your nerves boil, your blood pressure runs all over the map, how does that help? Where are those feelings going to be expressed? They have to come out somewhere or at someone.'

I was getting wound up, my passion bursting as I continued.

'I choose to help the way my heart directs me to help by loving to the best of my ability and being happy. Why? In order to serve every person Life brings to me. When I model love and happiness in the midst of chaos I provide shelter where others can catch their breath, gather their thoughts, and regroup. If they reconnect to themselves then they can serve in the way they are meant to serve, if they so choose.'

I stopped and looked at my husband who was quietly watching me. I'm not sure it was a look of disbelief, annoyance, or he really understood, but it didn't matter I continued.

'To me taking action, finding the calm in the storm is more important than reading about what has happened in the past. I honor the past by asking myself what I can do in the present to serve this world. Being present and living my life to the fullest is always the answer I hear.'

Joe looked at me without saying a word and went back to his newspaper. My thoughts swirled.

What if our happiness serves those around us in ways we never imagined? What if seeking happiness is the best thing we could do?

CONNECTING TO TRUTH

Do not go where the path may lead, go instead where there is no path and leave a trail.

Ralph Waldo Emerson

THOUGHTS weave in and out as I contemplate eternal questions. Why are we here? What is our purpose? No one has to talk me into believing the answers when I hear Truth. I know it. I have a master teacher who lives in my heart.

Accessing that teacher, recognizing that teacher's voice is tricky. How do I know if it's the still small voice of my master teacher?

First I must want to know my master teacher. Second, I must believe deep within me that the teacher exists and is Truth.

My drawer is filled with ideas, thoughts, rituals, mantras, affirmations, practices, religious teachings, books, and experiences that connect me with my master teacher.

What I put in my drawer must meet certain requirements. The requirements are that they must either connect me to my heart, bring out the best in me, make me happy, fan the passion of my purpose, help me know myself better, give me ways to heal, or expand my compassion and serve others.

Simple.

I've picked up numerous ideas over the years. I've used several of them many times, some less than others, and some I keep for future encounters.

My personal practice primarily follows my particular expression of eternal Truth, but I am open to learning about other ways to experience the Sacred. Each spiritual teacher I respect has the same message. Different words may be used, but it's the same message.

Love. Be kind to others. Serve your fellow human being. Respect the earth and all of its creatures.

The more I study, the more common threads I find. The more willing I am to learn the spiritual language used by others, the more I can, will, and do relate to individuals when they are in need. It serves to listen first and talk later.

As I listen with the ears of my heart I'm guided to their expression of eternal Truth. That allows me to speak with words that will not offend but resonate with their heart.

Listening to the heart reconnects us to Love.

ANSWERS

Be patient toward all that is unsolved in your
heart and try to love the questions themselves
like locked rooms and like books that are written
in a very foreign tongue.

Rainer Maria Rilke - Letters on Love

RY to live the questions. Be okay with today. In time all is revealed.

Whatever is stirring inside of me, let it steep like a good cup of herbal tea on a cold day or a sleepless night. Let me take the hot water to my lips slowly. I don't want to burn my tongue but I want the steaming liquid to drizzle into my mouth. When it's just right the warm cup becomes a coveted treasure grasped between my palms. I breathe in to the warmth and it immediately fogs my glasses.

Answers reveal themselves in their own time. Questions stimulate growth. Prayer and being present are what I take into the eye of the storm. Even if it looks like I'm doing nothing I am living the questions, doing the best I can, working with what I have.

FROM ONE MOTHER TO ANOTHER

If you're feeling lonely, take heart in the
sparks of life around you.

Tom Brown – Field Guide to Wilderness Survival

A friend of mine was dealing with the emotional
pain of having her daughter move out of state. Her
daughter had married and was moving across the
country. Before she got married she had lived with her
mother. Now she was leaving.

I could relate to my friend's situation so I sent her the
following e-mail.

Subject: From one mother to another

My Dear Friend,
Shifting relationships... pain, joy, sorrow, happiness...
oh how they dance in and out of each other. Mothers
and daughters weave their own web of love and
strength...
I was lucky during the transition periods with my
daughter, Desirae. Our first separation occurred when
she left home and moved into a dorm in Seattle to
attend the university. Sharp pangs of self doubt
loomed large. 'Will she ever need me', 'what use am I
now', 'I love her and miss her so much'. Self-

questioning went on and on. My daughter was forging her own identity, her own road without me.

The only thing that kept me going was my belief that God never does anything for only one reason. There is a multitude of reasons, meanings, plans, perspectives or outcomes for those of us willing to explore. My initial take always expands with time.

When my daughter left home my life was at a crossroads. Motherhood, my guiding, shaping, teaching role was shifting; not ending, but shifting. Desirae was ready to find her own way despite my resistance. It was time for her to experience her strength, to see how strong she truly is. That meant leaving me. Ouch, ouch, ouch.

My role changed. I had to move to the back seat even though I love to drive. I fought the change. I sulked, cried, and wanted her to need me like the old times. My vision was so blurred I didn't realize she needed me differently. More than my own neediness I wanted her to hold her own reins, so I did it, I moved to the back seat, and wondered if she would ever need me again.

After her graduation my daughter decided to follow her heart and move to California to venture out and see a new part of the world. Ouch again. We packed up her car and took a road trip to California. There I was, the one who wanted her home, or at least in Seattle. Yes, me, singing to the tunes cranked loud in her car. The sun was shining, her belongings in tow, it was really happening. She was moving. We stopped to take a picture of her standing next to the Entering California sign. Smiling, I took the picture as my heart was breaking.

Another shift, ouch. My heart was heavy. I wanted to scream, why can't she stay here? Then I heard the still small voice, 'would you really want her here? Didn't you raise her to follow her heart? Shouldn't she do what her heart sings for her to do? Isn't her happiness greater than your sorrow?'

'Yes', I shouted back. I want what's best for her, but please, God, hold me for I can barely stop the pain. I am breaking in two.

I am with you... the still small voice answered. I am with you.

Two years later she moved to the east coast. Me in Seattle, she back east, no quick flights in case she needs me. Yes, I know we are only a phone call away, but really, all the way across the country. Give me a break.

I heard the still small voice again, 'Sandy, do you believe your purpose was only to mother your daughter, do you believe that everything you tried to instill in your children was only for that reason, for that purpose? Open your eyes, my dear one'. The still small voice whispered, 'open your eyes, and see how I'm using you. You are my servant and I use you in magnificent ways. I always have. Don't you see what you do for me? Fear not my little one, for I am with you. I am guiding you, too.'

'OK, but why does this ride have to be so bumpy?' ...my heart cried through my tears.

My daughter's life became very busy with a new man, her new teaching job, her new friends, with everything but me. I had been holding on to the dream that one day she would move back home, that maybe this was a phase. I let go of that and gave it to God.

The every other day phone calls were replaced by the once a week call. Sometimes, depending on how exhausted I am or how disconnected I feel, I take it personally. I imagine she doesn't miss me, or worse that she doesn't need me and that her not calling is about me.

But then Life says, 'Stand back and look beyond your feelings and ask yourself is she happy? Isn't she experiencing everything you've always wanted for her?'

The answer is yes. I know my daughter loves me with all her heart, but more importantly she loves herself and her life. She is happy and her happiness takes precedence over my wanting her here.

Desirae and I have a very close long distance relationship. She sees me as often as she can and when we talk there is no distance between us. I am proud of her. She loves me and I love her. I am happy she is living the life of her dreams.

I have a purpose beyond the role of motherhood. God uses me in numerous ways, in more ways than I can see. I am meant to serve each person put in front of me. To serve in the best way I can. I forget sometimes and get in my own way, but my goal is to heal anything that stops me from doing what I believe I am meant to do, love.

I don't claim to know how you're feeling, but I want you to know from a mother who also loves her daughter more than anything. I send you love. I hope you can feel my hug. Nurture your sadness and love yourself extra special. You deserve it. You've done a great job.

Love, Sandy

AWARENESS

People have to be responsible for their thoughts, so they have
to learn to control them.

Rolling Thunder – Doug Boyd

I F we really monitored our thoughts, what would we
find? Way back when I challenged myself for one hour
I'd watch my thoughts. After a few minutes I was
exhausted. I found myself in trivia chaos. I did this
throughout the day for many days. Each little thought gave
me clues. I used them as steppingstones leading me to
happiness.

The Bible tells us the kingdom of God is within us, but
where? In our hearts? Between the blood vessels? Where is
it? If you can't dissect it or bring it out when you operate,
does that mean it's not there? Where is it? What is it? How
do we enter?

Awareness. When I started listening to myself talk and
paying attention, my life changed, slowly, but surely. With
awareness came choices. Doug Boyd in his book, *Rolling
Thunder*, says, 'First of all, if we don't want to think certain
things we don't say them. We don't have to eat everything
we see, and we don't have to say everything we think. So we
begin by watching our words and speaking with good
purpose only.'

In my old life I walked around in ignorance. Speaking out
or reacting based on how I was feeling. If I had an

appointment to go somewhere and didn't feel like going I didn't go. I'd call in sick or miss my appointment.

When I made the decision to find happiness I had to operate beyond the roller coaster of my emotions. Life became a daily battlefield. I struggled between what I felt like doing and doing what I knew was right for me.

One part of me seeks instant gratification and the other part of me knows better. I know what is healthy for my self-esteem and confidence. Happiness hinges on my courage and strength, the qualities it takes to operate from the part of me that knows.

Awareness opens doors you never knew existed.

ADDING GOOD THINGS

Thought is creative energy, and will automatically correlate with its object and bring it into manifestation.

Charles F. Haanel – The Master Key

CHANGE one ingredient and change the end product. We are the end product. One small simple thing changes us. Keep adding good things to your life and what isn't so good will fall away naturally. Only so much can fit into this tank called our body.

What do I call the small things I add to my life?

Steppingstones. Each thing we do leads us to our next experience. My dear sweet friend has a saying: 'believe, begin, become'. I agree. This book started with my belief that I was supposed to write it. I took action, wrote my first word, and eventually with a lot of perseverance it became what it is today, this book. Something was created out of nothing.

Or was it nothing? What if this book was hanging out somewhere waiting to be born? How many other thoughts are waiting to be born and brought to life? How many have I started and never finished?

My beliefs could be healthy and my thoughts pure, or they could be pitch black with mold growing on them. What I think I'm bound to experience. Think negative, negative happens; think positive, and positive will happen.

People don't give themselves a break. Negative thinking is habit forming. Bad habits are hard to break and good habits are hard to start. We hear the idea 'think positively and your life will be positive'. Then we recite one affirmation, think a few good thoughts, and if our life doesn't immediately transform, we think, hooey, that wasn't true. I was right all along, life sucks, the cards are stacked against me.

How many projects have I started and stopped because I didn't see the results fast enough. How many stars are in the sky?

Giving myself a break is essential. Pain kept under wraps works its way out in spurts of rage, or anger, or nasty remarks. I didn't realize those behaviors were caused from not listening to my pain. Instead, I'd blame others for my behavior.

When I kept adding one small good ingredient at a time, my life slowly filtered out all the unhealthy ingredients. There wasn't enough room for them. Bad relationships, bad habits didn't fit in the life I was creating. When I switched my energy from worrying about the negatives and trying to figure out how to fix them and refocused that energy on adding to my life, everything took care of itself.

Ingredients varied. Having a circle of intimate friends, a support team, eating healthier, getting exercise, journaling, seeing a counselor, going to a healer, letting myself play without being guilty, the list is so long that there's not enough room for all the good things I've added over the years.

All I know is good things flush out the 'yucky stuff' naturally. Change occurs when you add something new, good or bad. Change just takes the components and creates new experiences according to what we put into it. Life doesn't judge what we put in.

I vote for conscious change. Faith is the essential ingredient for conscious change. Start adding from there.

TURNING FIFTY

*I alone can improve myself and make myself more like the
person I would like to grow to be.*

Toni Morrison – I Dream A World –
Interview by Brian Lanker

THE day I turned fifty I felt different. I woke up with vivid dream images swirling in my head. Though they were good they were promptly forgotten as I brushed my teeth. It's a strange feeling, fifty. I've hit a milestone. No longer youthful. My time for excuses has expired.

I didn't feel bad. I felt mortal. A determined feeling was present. I decided right then that I would die trying, versus not trying at all. You'll never regret what you've tried; you'll only regret what you didn't try. These words I heard from a character on television last night. They stopped me cold. Trying to do what? I asked myself.

'Live life from the heart', my still small voice replied. Live your purpose. Step into the shoes you were born to wear.

There were no excuses for not stepping out and living life completely from the heart. No one was stopping me from trying. I was in the driver's seat, wasn't I?

My God, I'm ripe. I'm entering my early sage years. No amount of rejection can stop me. What others may think of my ideas or my attempts at getting those ideas out there doesn't matter. What matters is I try. It matters that I'm attempting to live life passionately and fully.

Joe and I talked about being fifty. We both feel a sense of peace as we herald this time of our lives. We imagine our fifties as being our best decade yet. We've worked hard to dance to our own music while breaking out of cultural pressures, from what's acceptable and what is not. Every day our intention is to live our purpose and we believe it's about to pay off.

We feel a sense of calm. We know each day is filled with chaos inside and out. But even when Life throws us a fireball, like Dorothy in the Wizard of Oz, we make it back to Kansas.

Sure, it takes the wind out of your sails when life knocks you down. But we have the courage, determination, and know-how to get back in the game and step back into happiness.

I printed out the first seventy pages of this manuscript and gave it to someone I love more than life and asked her to share what resonated with her and what didn't. She called me a week later and told me she was really disappointed with what I wrote. Boom. I was stunned. Endless hours I'd spent writing and rewriting and the first review was one of disappointment. It hurt.

I was knocked off balance for a couple of hours. In the past I would have hung up my writing gloves for years. Instead I tuned inward. I went up to my bathroom and looked at myself in the mirror. My heart looked back at me and told me, 'this is perfect, you will be rejected, not everyone will like what you write, many won't understand it and for some it won't be the right time.' Then I heard the deeper message: it is not your business to figure out who will be served by this book, your responsibility is to write what you believe you've been called to write. Leave the rest up to God.

186

Rejection at age fifty when turned inward reveals another purpose. Yes.

I'm different than I was when younger. I'm more authentic and more appreciative of the precious moments life offers. Joe and I miss our loved ones who have died and no longer grace our lives. Yet it is in the yearning to talk with them and kiss them one more time that makes us more determined to love each other and those around us to our best ability now.

On a flight to visit my friend recently, the plane's engine caught fire. We had to make an emergency landing. I was amazed at how calm I was. I called my husband from my cell phone while aboard the plane and told him what was going on. After reassuring him that the pilot had it under control, Joe commented that he was surprised how calm I was.

During the minutes of uncertainty I had thought about my life. I've had a good life. I am happy. I'm at peace. If I die on this plane, so be it, I thought. I didn't think I was going to die, but if I did I wasn't panicked.

I had no control over the situation. The only control I possessed was in my heart, what was happening on the outside of me I was helpless to fix.

Everything turned out okay but I surprised myself with the calmness that came over me. Others were scared. In fact, some were terrified. I heard them chattering away once we landed. I couldn't relate to what I was hearing because I was at peace. Wow, I thought, I love fifty.

Too bad that calmness isn't present when I'm riding in the car with my husband. There I still lose it. The pilot had no control over engine malfunction. All he could do was use his best professional effort to get us down. My husband, on the other hand, could slow down and back off the other cars. Yes, maybe even consider a class for road rage. I told him, probably more than once, I'll be mad if I die because you had road rage or didn't slow down. Okay, I admit it. I still have work to do.

LISTENING

The deeper one sees into life, the wider life opens itself to one,
and every moment of one's life then becomes full of wonders
and full of splendour.

Inayat Khan – Music

LISTENING is an art. There are so many books describing the transformational qualities of listening. If we all learned how to listen we'd become angels on earth forever.

My first task was to shut up, to get rid of my own agenda. When I did my heart gave me exactly the right thing to say and do. I didn't have to think my way through the experience of listening.

Hospice training anchored me in the art of listening. It's not about you. It's about them. They are the teachers. You will learn from those you are blessed to serve. Be a presence. My hospice boss said, 'if you've said more than five things, you've said too much. Listen.'

It was hard to shut up. For years I felt that no one listened to me so when I got the opportunity to talk it came out fast and furious. Words tumbled out before I had a chance to string them together. I'd jump ahead trying to figure out the answer while barely hearing what was being said.

Some people are so kind; they let you ramble on and on.

If my old listening style served a purpose I just wonder how much more could have been accomplished if I had left

189

my agenda at home. It was wrong thinking it was my job to have the answers. My job was to listen.

Who was I tuned in to, them or me?

People would tell me how much they got from our talks but when I discovered the art of listening our sessions got deeper. I was out of my own way. Don't think, I told myself, be present and listen. I'd make myself clear my mind and tune in to the person in front of me. Listen to the words with the ears of my heart was my motto.

To be listened to is powerful.

When I need someone to listen to me what I don't need is someone giving me advice. It drives me batty when someone tells me that I need this or that before I've finished talking. How do they know what I need? All I need is to be heard.

No words of wisdom will sink in when there's no more room inside of me. I'm filled to the brim. I've got to unload some of my thoughts in order to let new ones in. When I'm overloaded I've got to vent. Please let me. Don't give me words or suggestions or remedies. Give me a hug.

Bless those who've learned how to listen.

PERCEPTIONS

To straighten the crooked you must first do a harder thing –
Straighten yourself.

Buddha – Dhammapada: The Sayings of the Buddha - Thomas
Byrom

CHANGING your perceptions will change your life.
I think of perceptions like sunglasses, you can have
a dozen of them. How you perceive something
isn't the whole truth and nothing but the truth. Change
your lenses and what do you see?

I've had experiences I didn't want to replay in my head
but, when it is time, I pull one out and lo and behold my
perception of the experience has shifted. Why? One reason is
my willingness to look at the experience through the eyes of
my heart, a process that seems to change things from bad to
better.

I'm glad healing happens in teaspoons because some
experiences are too painful to look at right away. Learning to
love myself and strengthen my confidence before dipping
back into the pit of pain is essential. When the time is right,
painful memories make their way to the surface. Slowly,
nurturing myself every step of the way I release them from
bondage.

I'm a logical person. I use the left side of my brain as much
as the right side. You need to use both to be on the road to
happiness. I thought that if I have only so much time each
day and I want to spend it in love and not tied up in knots, I

better figure out what's stopping me. What I discovered was unresolved hurts. What I did was heal.

Being introspective serves me well. I check each day to determine if I've spent most of my time worrying, feeling down, or unappreciated. If so, then something needs addressing.

There is always something behind the curtain of emotion. Nothing is black and white. If you think it is you are not looking at the experience with the eyes of your heart. Potential opportunities for happiness lay dormant in every experience.

When it comes to childhood I bet my siblings and parents have an altogether different take on my experiences. It took a lot of nurturing and getting stronger to realize others in my experiences wore sunglasses too. Their lenses were different from mine. If theirs were green and mine were pink, maybe their version of an experience looked different. I wasn't denying my version, but was opening to the possibility that their version existed.

I lived what 'I lived'. I also believe they lived what 'they lived'. Fighting over who was right, what should have been and why it wasn't is pointless. It's wasted energy trying to determine which version is true. We're both right. No one can turn back the clock to change what happened. We both experienced what we experienced.

When I stopped wasting time to focus on healing things started to happen. Getting my story out and putting it on the table is my only way to heal. By doing that I make space to explore the possibility that other versions exist and if they exist, how could that possibility help me heal?

Who I tell my story to is important. It has to be an individual with the capacity to be present and who knows how to listen. Over the years it's been a friend, or family member, or even a stranger I meet having coffee. When I'm ready to talk, life sends me the right person.

Making room to expand my perceptions is the best thing I ever did. Now, whenever I think I know something, I make it a habit to ask, 'what if there is more here than what meets the eye? Is there another way to see this, another version of the story? What if...'

STARTING AGAIN

Be taken up and cast into the sea,
it will be done. And whatever
you ask for in prayer, having faith and really
believing, you will receive.

Matthew 21:21-22

LOSING my job was scary. Fearful of not being able to pay our mortgage or finding the resources to pay for health insurance, and the thought of not being able to help my children if they needed me made me sick. The worst thought of all was the possibility of having to take a full time job doing something I didn't want to do.

My old job was comfortable. It allowed me to work on my calling at the same time I got a paycheck and health insurance. It was a safety net in case my calling didn't work out.

Was I living my faith by having a safety net or by doing something half-heartedly? Who said I had to get a regular job to pay the bills? Where was it written that one must seek employment in a field they don't like?

I don't know why I thought serving half-heartedly was serving. My greatest desire was to break free from my job and serve God full time. I recognized my yearning to serve, a yearning that grows stronger the older I get. It had been pressing on my heart for some time, the time was here. Why was I scared?

195

I have always been introspective, sensitive. I used to read about the Catholic saints and get excited. When I was a kid I even helped clean the convent where the nuns lived in order to be around those mysterious women so dedicated to God.

I have the ability to love deeply and stand in a place of Truth. Being with others and helping them as they step into the shoes they were born to wear is my passion. But they don't sell instruction kits on how to survive doing that, and that's why I kept my safe job and told myself I was building towards my calling. Wasn't that good enough?

When it sank in that I had no job, a mini-nervous breakdown quickly ensued. It took place in my driveway as I stood out in the rain washing my car. But before I tell you about that I need to give you some background.

Earlier in the day after a phone call from my former boss and having been laid off I left for my part-time job at the local community college to teach a class feeling stunned. Half way there I looked over to the passenger's seat and noticed my backpack wasn't there. No backpack meant no lecture notes. I didn't even remember leaving my house. Did I bring the backpack to my car? Did I put it on the trunk while I unlocked the door? Was it on the side of the road somewhere? I had no clue.

I couldn't remember if I'd put our eight year old Lab back in the house. Maybe she was outside with no way to get back in. Maybe she was dead on the road hit by a car. I was over half way to school with no time to go back.

With my head pounding and my stomach in knots I walked into the classroom donning my happy face. Isn't that what good teachers are supposed to do? Put on a happy face, leave our problems at home, and be there for those in front of us? I asked if I could borrow a textbook so I could try and remember my lecture notes.

Towards the end of class my blood sugar was dipping. My stomach churned and my head ached. I was supposed to start a new women's group for the Women's Services Department later that afternoon, but I knew I had to cancel. How could I start a new group feeling like that? I had no energy, nothing to give. I was empty, completely drained.

Class ended. As I was about to walk out the door four women from class asked, 'Isn't today the day you start your new group?'

Hiding my problems with a half smile I nodded and said, 'Yes, and it would be great to see you there,' as I rushed out the door.

Was I nuts? What did I just do? What is wrong with me?

I needed food so I headed for the store to get something to eat. I told myself I had an hour before group started so eat and you'll feel better. I drove to the supermarket, went into the deli, got a salad. Then I sat in my car trying to force a few bites down, but couldn't. Yes I need to diet, but really, this isn't the way.

I put the food on the passenger seat, tilted my seat back, and sat staring out the windshield at a gray sky. There wasn't one cloud, just a blanket of gray everywhere.

'What am I going to do?' I asked myself. I'm supposed to lecture about how to listen to the Sage within. How can I teach that when I feel so disconnected? As I tried deep breathing to put my headache into remission my heart spoke to me, 'Don't you think how disconnected you feel would be a great way to start the class?'

I sat up and looked out the window staring at nothing. I closed my eyes and rolled the idea around in my head.

Maybe that's what I'm supposed to do. I prayed, if this is your will, so be it.

A peace came over me, I still felt ill, but I felt sharing my experience was right.

When I walked into the workshop room I expected to see about eight or so attendees. Instead the room was nearly full. I smiled and acknowledged each person in their seat. At the same time I was trying to compose myself, waiting for the clock to strike noon and the class to start. When it was time, I thanked every one for being there, looked at them in silence. Then I told them my earlier intention had been to cancel the workshop.

It seemed like the whole room groaned. They looked at each other, then one by one started telling me how glad they were that I didn't cancel. They said they had been looking forward to the group all month and how they had heard me last year, or a friend told them about me. As their words tumbled out, my heart softened.

I explained why I was going to cancel. I told them I lost my full-time job about three hours ago and I was scared; in fact terrified. I said I didn't know what I was going to do and felt I didn't have it in me to do the group. I told them about my trip to the supermarket, sitting in my car and staring at the sky when suddenly I heard my heart suggest that I tell you my story.

I reminded them that this session was about listening to the Sage within and how I was sure my Sage within had skipped town. And then I told the class that as I sat alone in my car in the parking lot I heard my heart say that this story is exactly what I need to share.

The group continued and each person opened up. We identified the things that stop us from hearing the still small

198

voice, our inner Sage, and what we can do to overcome those obstacles. We shared from the heart and, as the hour concluded, I realized my headache was gone, my sadness had lifted and my energy was soaring.

It was as if Life was affirming that indeed facilitating groups, speaking, living life from the heart was exactly what I was supposed to do. I was more determined than ever to make that happen full time in my life.

Filled to the brim I left the workshop and within a few hours I was standing in my driveway having a mini-nervous breakdown. It was crazy to wash my car in the rain, but I had to. Maybe it was symbolic, I don't know. All I do know is I had to wash my dirty car. I let loose in my driveway every emotion. With tears, runny nose, wet hair, and hands dipping into the cold sudsy water, I screamed into the overcast sky, cursing Life, certain I was a lunatic washing her car, but what could I do.

I had turned into the neighborhood crazy woman. I needed to be nuts, I realize now, to empty my pain. My tears cleansed me.

Later that night in bed I reflected on the day. The highs of the workshop and the lows of the breakdown. What was I being prepared for? Whatever it was, the time was now.

Scanning the afternoon scene in my mind as I lay in bed with my sleeping husband I remembered seeing something out of the corner of my eye while I was in the driveway. Our neighbor's horse was watching me. Normally the horse can't make it to the gate closest to our house, but there he stood. His ears alert pointed toward me as I had my tantrum. Those big brown eyes staring at me. Had God used the horse to calm me in the midst of my pain? If so, I couldn't believe it, but it was true. While lying in bed the serenity and love I felt from this beautiful creature was overwhelming.

My Kleenex box got a work out as I thought back on the day. I gave thanks knowing how much I'm loved. I was grateful for the horse and for losing my job. I was grateful for the women in the workshop and how they had served me more than I served them. Life never ceases to amaze me. I am taken care of, always. Losing my job was not an ending, it was a beginning, a starting over.

It was time to embrace my purpose with both arms. No more pussy-footing around. I was empty and ready to be filled by God. To know there is no going back is liberating. There will be no more half-hearted efforts. I am freefalling into God's arms and trusting I will be shown the way.

CONCLUSION

Will I ever find a resting spot?
Or is everyplace I go another steppingstone?
Am I meant to wander with no spiritual home, no label, only
undying love for God? Or is each steppingstone the resting
spot I seek?

AFTERWORD

Dear great, great, great grandchild,

The words in this book were written before you were born. Although we have never met I feel I know you deeply. Our outer worlds may look different, but the inner landscape we share is the same.

When I first felt the urge to write I wouldn't show the manuscript to anyone. I wrote every day. The letters fell onto the page creating an opening to my inner world, a sacred place I cherish inside of me. I wasn't sure why I was writing. I wondered who would want to read these words, yet I knew they were meant for someone. I felt an urge to keep going, to reveal my journey, my pains, my sorrows, my joys, and yes, my happiness.

One day when the manuscript was done I asked a friend her thoughts on why I wrote this book. She said, 'What if this book is for your great, great, great grandchild? What if he or she needs what you're writing?' As soon as those words were spoken I knew it was true. This book was written for you.

You needed me and I'm here. I'm here to let you know I made it out of my brokenness and found happiness. It is my intention to serve you. You, my dear one, deserve to be happy.

I believe in you. You may not be able to touch me in the flesh, but you've already touched me in my heart. We are connected beyond comprehension.

We are one.

I will love you forevermore,
Your Devoted Grandmother

ENDNOTES

I have gathered books and quotes throughout my lifetime. If sources have not been credited correctly, please notify us. Every effort will be made to correct future printings.

QUOTATIONS ARE FROM:

Bible – Different versions used throughout the book
Gift from the Sea – Anne Morrow Lindbergh
Letters on Love – Rainer Maria Rilke
Quiet Thoughts – Paul S. McElroy
Voices of a People's History of the United States – Howard
   Zinn - Chief Joseph Recounts His Trip to Washington D.C.
   (1879)
I Dream A World – Interviews by Brian Lanker
My Lord Love A Pure Heart – Swami Chidvilasanada
The Gift: Poems by Hafiz - translations by Daniel Ladinsky
ReImagining Christianity – Alan Jones PhD
Sabbath – Wayne Muller
The Prophet – Kahlil Gibran
As A Man Thinketh – James Allen
Legacy of the Heart – Wayne Muller
Medicine Wheels: Ancient Teachings for Modern Times –
   Roy I. Wilson
Celebration of Discipline – Richard J. Foster
The Essence of Self-Realization – Paramhansa Yogananda
God Is A Verb – Rabbi David A. Cooper
Think and Grow Rich – Napoleon Hill
Journey of Desire – John Eldredge

In Love – Stephen C. Paul

Toward a Meaningful Life: The Wisdom of the Rebbe
  Menachem Mendel Schneerson – Simon Jacobson

Called to Question – Joan Chittister

First You Have To Row A Little Boat – Richard Bode

Play to Win – Larry Wilson and Hersch Wilson

We Can't Teach What We Don't Know – Gary Howard

Outside Lies Magic: Regaining History & Awareness in
  Everyday Places – John Stilgoe

The Master Key – Charles F. Haanel

Rolling Thunder – Doug Boyd

Art of Happiness – His Holiness the Dalai Lama

The Inner Voice of Love: A Journey Through Anguish to
  Freedom – Henri J.M. Nouwen

OTHER AUTHORS & BOOKS ...

Henri Nouwen - Anything written by Fr. Nouwen will open
  your heart.

Marsha Sinetar - a pioneering educator and excellent author.
  Her tapes and books continue to mentor me.

Tao Te Ching - Different translations continue to stimulate
  and expand my awareness.

Streams In The Desert: 366 Daily Devotional Readings – L.B.
  Cowman – This Christian devotional I've turned to many
  times. It reconnects me to my heart when I need it.

Pema Chodron - a Buddhist nun in the Tibetan vajrayana
  tradition. Her way of teaching is deep and practical. Her
  books on tape have been music to my ears for many years.

J. Krishnamurti - His tapes and books are direct and provoke
  questions about daily life.